C000129766

CREATING THE
HIGH
PERFORMANCE
WORK PLACE

IT'S NOT COMPLICATED
TO DEVELOP A
CULTURE OF COMMITMENT

SUE BINGHAM & BOB DUSIN

 INDIE BOOKS
INTERNATIONAL

Copyright © 2018 by HPWP Group

All rights reserved.

Printed in the United States of America.

No part of this publication may be reproduced or distributed in any form or by any means without the prior permission of the publisher. Requests for permission should be directed to permissions@ indiebooksintl.com, or mailed to Permissions, Indie Books International, 2424 Vista Way, Suite 316, Oceanside, CA 92054

Neither the publisher nor the author is engaged in rendering legal or other professional services through this book. If expert assistance is required, the services of appropriate professionals should be sought. The publisher and the author shall have neither liability nor responsibility to any person or entity with respect to any loss or damage caused directly or indirectly by the information in this publication.

ISBN-10: 1-947480-18-9
ISBN-13: 978-1-947480-18-6
Library of Congress Control Number: 2018940379

Designed by Joni McPherson, mcphersongraphics.com

Additional Copyright and Trademark Reference
High Performance Leadership Workshop™ is a trademark of HPWP Consulting, LLC.

All the stories in this book are inspired by true events. The names and identifying details have been changed to protect privacy. Any resemblance to actual persons or organizations is purely coincidental.

TABLE OF **CONTENTS**

Foreword v

Breaking Tradition 1

Introduction 3

    Chapter 1: The Genesis of the High-Performance Work Place . . 5

    Chapter 2: Feeling the Heat 13

    Chapter 3: A Better Way 17

The High Performance Culture 23

    Chapter 4: Lead With Positive Assumptions 25

    Chapter 5: Identify and Eliminate Negatives 41

    Chapter 6: Build Trust and Mutual Respect 57

    Chapter 7: Practice Open, Two-Way, Adult-to-Adult
    Communication 69

    Chapter 8: Engage and Involve Employees 83

    Chapter 9: Conduct Exceptional Training 95

    Chapter 10: Ensure Competitive Wages and Benefits 107

    Chapter 11: Establish High Expectations 121

Making It Happen 139

About the Authors 149

Acknowledgments 151

Works Cited 153

FOREWORD

Sue and Bob asked me to write a forward for this book and address how the HPWP concepts came about. I thought *there's no easy way to explain the mixed-up combination of early life experiences, but I'll try....*

Working in a truck stop during my teen years I learned that, in a low profit business, everyone was required to do everything—mopping floors, changing truck tires, tracking inventory, dealing with drunks at 3:00 in the morning, whatever. I learned that being self-managed was pretty much the only option, that working with peers was the only way to accomplish all the work that was needed to get done and that laughing a lot (I mean *a lot*) made the job fun. Individual responsibility and accountability were a given.

As I grew older I worked in a series of factory jobs. I was a very young husband and father, and income was critical. I wanted to make enough money to care for my family and be able to continue my education. I learned my personal needs had nothing whatsoever to do with the company's needs. Being a "replacement part" is too charitable a way to describe my experiences. I was let go from each of these jobs for different reasons and with no conversation:

"Laid off." (What? I worked harder than anyone there.)

"Workers' comp risk." (What? I only said lifting these 80-pound hot dirty tires made my back sore.)

"Refusal to follow instructions." (What? After checking 3,000 of these little plastic pieces, what's the matter with using a sampling approach?)

After college, I was blessed to work for a large employer with plants across the nation. I was provided extensive opportunities and an exceptional mentor, Don Cisek. While I had the exalted title of Personnel Administrative Assistant, I was treated from the very first as a contributing and valued team member. I was included in decision making that was far beyond that for which I felt qualified. I was given work that I initially was certain I couldn't do. I was "promoted" to bag carrier for the executives that were negotiating labor agreements. I'd already learned the value of responsibility, accountability and hard work. During this time, I learned that an underlying goal was for everyone to win; that communication included listening and certainly has to be two-way; that trust and respect were critical; and that paying a fair and competitive wage was in everyone's best interest. I learned that being involved creates ownership and loyalty. I discovered that the most motivating and rewarding aspect of work was being valued. But most importantly, I found that *doing the right thing was always the right thing.*

I continued to learn through a series of work assignments that included the need to be exceptionally analytical (those that know me are not even trying to contain their laughter). I saw in my organization and in other traditional companies that people were treated differently based on the work they performed—not only factory as compared to office but administrative compared to management and midlevel management as compared to executives. These differences were demonstrated in day-to-day interaction, policy and rule applications, benefits and opportunities for involvement and development. It became clear that making a smaller percentage of employees more satisfied while creating dissatisfaction for a larger percentage of employees in the same company is always a mistake.

In this book Sue and Bob talk about a significant assignment I had that led to the elements of a high-performance work place. These elements are no doubt critical to an organization's success. It is, however, the common sense practical application of these elements in conjunction with valuing employees and doing the right thing that leads to exceptional performance.

It really isn't complicated.

Ken Bingham

BREAKING
TRADITION

INTRODUCTION

The value of each employee's unique and individual character is often eclipsed by the fear of litigation and working in an era of corporate arrogance. It's no secret that there will soon be more jobs and fewer people to fill them. The coming generations who will fill these jobs will not easily fit into a company and culture that doesn't provide them with purpose and development and value. It's time to get back to leading with common sense and kindness. Leaders must challenge how they lead people today instead of blindly accepting traditional management practices. What we know today warns us that this prevalent approach will not stand the test of a changing workforce and the changing nature of work itself.

The good news is there is an uncomplicated alternative to this dated management approach that is startling in its simplicity and rewarding in its results. We start with the genesis of the philosophy after which we have named our business—the High Performance Work Place (HPWP). It was created over thirty years ago by Ken Bingham and has been continually enhanced through real-time, hands-on implementation. Some of what is presented in this book may be challenging to many who are content with a familiar, traditional working environment. While challenging, it is not complicated for smart, extremely capable leaders to adopt this common-sense approach, and it is highly likely these principles will support such leaders' values.

HPWP is comprised of eight elements. These elements are all worthwhile principles that should form the foundation of any successful organization's work culture. However, as the applications of these elements are illustrated, some leaders may be skeptical that such a workplace is realistic today. It is.

When you have finished this book, you will look at yourselves and the workplace with new eyes—inspired to make a difference in the lives of the people with whom you work, as well as in your own life.

CHAPTER **1**
The Genesis of the High-Performance Work Place

From his early thirties until his retirement, Ken Bingham has devoted his career to finding and fine-tuning elements that create the highest-performing work environments. By doing so, he has, directly and indirectly, impacted thousands of people's lives, both at their workplaces and in their homes. He has done this through his own high standards for hard work and excellence as well as by applying these same expectations to everyone around him. He calls his system the *High Performance Work Place*, or HPWP. In the simplest of terms, he would describe this as, "Do the Right Thing—Every Time."

If you have seen the standup comedy routines of Jerry Seinfeld, you know he makes us all aware of how humorously stupid our commonly accepted thoughts and behaviors are. That's also Ken. He is extremely impatient with policies, practices, and decisions that don't make sense. Driven by the dual desire to make the companies he has worked for successful and the people with whom he worked feel valued, Ken developed the philosophy and applications in the following pages. Everything we know today about creating the most successful workplaces comes from being his devoted apprentices.

Researching High-Performing Companies

Over thirty years ago, Ken worked for CECO, a major construction company, with over seventy locations throughout the country. CECO's businesses consisted of steel mills, manufacturing plants, construction sites, and supporting warehouses and facilities. Over 80 percent of the operations were unionized, involving over fifty different labor agreements.

Do the Right Thing— Every Time.

While CECO was very strong in the construction business at that time, the company was experiencing losses in market share in some of its manufacturing lines. Executive leadership was dissatisfied with the current situation and was alarmed looking at forecasts for the future. They determined that, while they could gain a competitive advantage through technology, innovation, automation, sales approaches, material utilization, and customer service, all these advantages would only prove temporary. Over time, the competition would be able to find and adopt similar techniques.

80 percent of what any organization does can be done equally well by any other organization.

Therefore, competitive success depends upon the other 20 percent— which is the people.

They considered and discussed the possibilities of a management style, or work environment, that would maximize productivity and reduce costs while avoiding unions and associated restrictive labor agreements.

Ken's job at the time was to negotiate many of the numerous labor agreements that were in place as well as monitor employee relations at the nonunion facilities. He was about to get an opportunity that would change his business life—and his personal life.

His assignment was to lead a small team to see if they could determine what principles were required to create the most productive work environment possible. The team met with companies throughout the country that were known for the best performance (or at least had a reputation for such) within each company's industry. After visiting and studying individual sites, team members collected information that began to coalesce into related concepts. Their conclusions formed the basis of the eight elements we will review in this book.

Soon CECO built a new facility in Milan, Tennessee, with a culture based completely on the recommendations of Ken's group. The facility would manufacture metal doors and doorframes. The product line would use machinery and equipment that was identical to that used in its Cicero, Illinois location.

The plant manager and production management team were selected from other company facilities. Their selection was based primarily on leadership skills, not on experience in operations. All the production employees and most of the support staff were hired locally. Extensive training was completed even before the doors opened. After six months of operation, the product line was out-performing the Cicero line by 100 percent. After one year of production, the Tennessee line was performing at over 200 percent of the Cicero line. In addition, the Milan plant had a long waiting list of applicants who wanted to work there, a turnover rate below 4 percent, and an absentee rate of less than

0.5 percent. The cost savings and resulting profits were phenomenal. CECO went on to start up several additional plants with this cultural approach and without the need or threat of union intervention.

So, why is a proven concept that works this well, and has been around for decades in many different forms, not practiced by most companies and organizations? The reasons will become apparent throughout this book as the high-performance road map is laid out.

It's Not Rocket Science

As organizations grow, they become more complex and bureaucratic. But think about small company startups where everyone does any job necessary. Employees may work long hours, but they are challenged and motivated to be successful. There aren't a lot of rules or policies. There is high trust. There is collaborative teamwork. High expectations are continually set, and they don't even need to be communicated. Job descriptions are not necessary, and no formal performance appraisal process exists. Everyone has access to the information, tools, and supplies that are required. It is hard to identify a manager—or even the owner—in the group. It is fun, and it is personally rewarding.

Company growth doesn't require abandoning all those characteristics of a great workplace. Companies absolutely need structure and communication when there is growth. But the pendulum often swings too far into bureaucracy and risk mitigation, and this begins to kill what made it successful in the first place (more about that later).

It's Not a Program

With the best of motives and a desire to pursue excellence, myriad management programs have been introduced to a workforce that has become more and more cynical toward any type of leadership training. The workforce has repeatedly seen initiatives begin with a lot of energy and end with barely a whimper. There's nothing wrong with many programs, which generally focus attention on improvement opportunities outside the whirlwind of the workday. Some are touted only to be successful if their implementation becomes part of the company culture. While this may occasionally happen, many of these programs rarely achieve that level of sustainability.

An employee of an HPWP client recently reduced all the complex explanations of culture by simply saying, "It's the way we do things around here." Culture is how decisions are made, challenges are faced, and problems are handled. When visiting any organization, the culture can be felt. As you walk through a facility, employees working in a high-performance culture are welcoming to visitors. They smile and wave while continuing to work; there is electricity in the air and a strong sense of unity. You can frequently hear laughter. Conversely, you can also feel the culture in an organization in which employees have become survivors or worse—zombies. They don't look up. The pace is moderate at best, there are no smiles, and eyes are figuratively and literally on the clock as it slowly marches toward the end of the day.

What HPWP Is

When managers commit to engaging common sense and judgment, creating a high-performance workplace is absolutely a competitive strategy. That's because a HPWP is:

- a *philosophy* that believes people are an organization's competitive edge,
- a *culture* that drives behaviors and decisions based on common values,

- an *operating system* that supports that culture,

- a *platform* for facilitating continuous growth and improvement, and

- a *legacy* for multi-generational family business leaders.

It's a place where people *want to come to work.*

A Leader's Scorecard

For over twenty-five years, the HPWP Group has conducted High Performance Leadership Workshops designed to help participants look at themselves and the people they work with in a more honest way—with positive assumptions *and* high expectations. As part of exploring workplace challenges, we've asked management participants six questions. The answers have been consistent for almost three decades, and they paint a picture of what we know and of what opportunities exist for significant improvements. Take a moment and answer these questions based on your current organization.

The Six Questions	Your Answer
1. How many people who work in your organization are good, responsible people (own homes, raise children, want to do the right thing)?	_____ percent
2. How much of each employee's potential do you (as an organization) use?	_____ percent
3. How much brainpower is required for most jobs?	_____ percent
4. In any given day, not including breaks and lunch, how much time per employee is nonproductive?	_____ hours
5. Who generally knows the job best—the supervisor or the employee?	_____
6. If a manager leaves his office, approaches an employee, asks him to come back to the office and shuts the door, what do you think is happening?	_____

Let's see how your responses compare to the responses of most of our participants.

1. How many people who work in your organization are good, responsible people (own homes, raise children, want to do the right thing)? Typical answer: *75-95 percent*

2. How much of each employee's potential do you (as an organization) use? Typical answer: *50 percent*

3. How much brainpower is required for most of the jobs? Typical answer: *30-60 percent*

4. In any given day, not including breaks and lunch, how much time per employee is nonproductive? Typical answer: *2 hours*

5. Who generally knows the job best—the supervisor or the employee? Typical answer: *The employee*

6. If a manager leaves his office, approaches an employee, asks him to come back to the office and shuts the door, what do you think is happening? Typical answer: *The employee is in trouble or did something wrong. It's something negative.*

You can see from these answers that managers and leaders believe that most employees are good, responsible people. However, organizations are using only half of their potential, and the jobs are not structured to maximize brainpower. At least 25 percent of each employee's day is nonproductive. Leaders believe the person doing the job every day knows it best, yet whenever they have any meaningful communication, the perception is often that the employee is in some type of trouble.

What a fantastic opportunity to improve and grow. At the very least, based on these answers, organizations should be able to do the same amount of work with 25 percent fewer people. This nonproductive time is not necessarily attributable to people avoiding their responsibilities. It also includes downtime caused by waiting for answers, approvals, and decisions; changes in schedules, systems; and procedures; equipment repair and maintenance; and unclear expectations.

This scorecard says that many companies are not maximizing their human capabilities. It's like spending a lot of money for a great operating system or piece of equipment, then using only a small percentage of its capacity.

CHAPTER **2**
Feeling the Heat

Most people don't change because they see the light—they change because they feel the heat. Organizations are identifying the need to attract and retain talent as one of the biggest business challenges today; they're starting to feel the heat. And that heat will intensify as the baby boomers retire at the rate of 10,000 per day, being replaced with a millennial generation that is fewer in number by 20 million, who have far different expectations. At the very least, millennials want to work for companies that give them a sense of purpose, challenging assignments, personal attention, and a variety of opportunities to learn and grow. They expect and want a balance between work and leisure. Despite these facts, and feeling the heat, organizations are not changing quickly enough.

What's getting in the way?

Obstacles to Creating a High-Performance Culture

Three obstacles significantly interfere with a company's, and a leader's, ability to effectively implement and live the elements of high performance.

1. Fear of Litigation

A leader's job is to create an environment where people thrive. Fear of litigation causes most larger companies to do the opposite. This fear is enhanced every time a class-action lawsuit or jury award against a company makes local and national headlines.

The HPWP approach absolutely respects the foundation upon which our laws have been built; there should be equal opportunity for everyone. People should expect to work in an environment free of harassment. Necessary laws are in place to keep workplaces safe. But there's a difference between ethical business practices and stifling bureaucracy.

Seeking to minimize risk, companies adopt and administer countless policies designed to catch the small percentage of bad apples. Here's the deal. Bad apples, if they get in the door, are going to cost a company no matter what rules are in place. But what is worse than having rules is the admonition that we need to treat everyone the same. When a solid contributor makes a reasonable request or makes a mistake and is treated the same as a laggard who is just trying to get away with something, the contributor is dehumanized. Treating everyone the same causes people to lose any sense of uniqueness and value. It translates to, "I'm just a number" and causes potential high performers to move into a zombie state—a mode of compliance rather than commitment. It's hard for leaders to truly know the cost of devaluing a person's contributions when the focus is on avoiding a big headline.

Companies who treat people fairly and strive to do the right things rarely find themselves in those headlines. HPWP companies can defend themselves from lawsuits without creating a stifling bureaucracy.

2. Thinking That a Top-Down, Autocratic Approach Still Works

Does it? Will it? It can be difficult to advise a company's senior leadership on the importance of engagement and empowerment when, by most measures, the company is successful. But consider how much more effective and successful a traditional company could be with a change in its leadership style and culture. Also, the autocratic management style that worked in the past is a miscalculated approach today, and for that very same reason, autocratic organizations are beginning to feel the heat.

3. The Perception that Culture is Fuzzy Stuff

Peter Drucker's well-known quote, "Culture eats strategy for breakfast," has become a popular phrase that many senior leaders believe to be true. There are meetings focused on markets, sales numbers, financials, products, production, shipments, customer service, logistics, schedules, and new business ventures. Most of these and other meetings focus on *what* has happened or needs to happen, supported by data. But how many meetings are ever scheduled simply to discuss the quality of the company culture? Culture is the framework that focuses on *how* a company accomplishes its *what*.

Organizations realize, now more than ever, that a continual and unwavering focus on culture as a business initiative is the key to sustaining future success.

CHAPTER 3
A Better Way

When a leader is trusted, those whom the leader influences go above and beyond standard expectations. When people have high levels of trust, they will commit to a path that may not be comfortable, and they will take risks. They will give their best out of respect for their leaders. So, what gets in the way of a strong trust environment in the workplace?

Almost always, it's the employee who is a bad apple.

Whether you are a teacher, a retail clerk, a production manager, or a doctor, you've dealt with the person who is trying to get something more in a devious or underhanded way. That is someone who can't be trusted.

Leaders usually spend more time dealing with bad apples than they do with the rest of their employees, either trying to change them or to find a way to get them out of the company. And based on these negative experiences, leaders tend to see the entire group through a tainted lens. Leaders also create rules and processes to try to "catch" and remove that small percentage of people who create the highest percentage of the negative impact. What a monumental waste of time.

HPWP is grounded in the belief that 95 percent of people are good people. Some will say it's less; some will say it's even more, but let's go with 95 percent. That leaves 5 percent of the workforce who are harmful to the organization. HPWP uses a very straightforward (and highly original) term for this group: Five-percenters.

We must be careful in applying this label too quickly. "Five-percenter" does not refer to people who may be struggling with a performance issue, resisting change, or challenging a management directive. A five-percenter is defined as:

- Someone whose motives are not good
- Someone whose goal is to do as little as possible as often as possible
- Someone who is not a team player
- Someone who is not trustworthy

Leaders know who these five-percenters are. Based on the definition, you can most likely name someone you know or have worked with that fits this description. You wouldn't want them as friends, and you don't want them as part of your organization. However, because many companies' hiring practices are archaic, leaders often end up with one or more five-percenters in their midst. Then they spend a lot of time trying to get rid of them. This grueling process impacts everyone—particularly the ninety-five-percenters.

HPWP starts with this foundational belief:

- Approximately 95 percent of all employees are responsible, good people
- Management resources have focused on protecting companies from the 5 percent, marginal-employee group
- This has a negative impact on the 95 percent

Review your policy manual. Are most policies written to catch the five-percenter? And can you see how these policies negatively impact the ninety-five-percenters? An example is a policy that states that an employee cannot receive holiday pay if he or she is absent the day before or day after the holiday. This policy was created, of course, to catch the person who falsely calls in sick to make a long weekend. Yet many managers and supervisors have known a great employee who actually *was* sick, or had an accident, or some other issue that was a legitimate reason for missing work the day before or after a holiday. Because they knew the employee and trusted the person, they felt it was wrong to penalize the employee by docking holiday pay. Some managers feel constrained by this type of policy, and these policies can make them feel and look powerless. Others simply find a way around the policy.

Ken Bingham negotiated labor agreements for seventeen years in his first professional job. He said that almost all the language in any labor contract is a result of either management abuse or employee abuse. In fact, during negotiations, people could recall the name of the person who had committed the abuse. Policies and contracts created to prevent or catch undesirable behavior are just a few of the factors that contribute to a grim work environment. And the application of these policies, rules, and contracts diminishes the value of the 95 percent (or more) of the great people who are unique individuals and often high-performing contributors.

For now, that's enough about the five-percenters; we've spent too much time on them already.

The Eight Key Elements

What Ken and his team learned, through studying the most respected and successful companies, and the resulting tested applications, has ultimately resulted in eight elements that will transform a traditional organization into a high-performance workplace:

1. Positive assumptions about people
2. Identification and elimination of negatives
3. Mutual trust and respect
4. Open, two-way, adult-to-adult communication
5. Employee involvement and empowerment
6. Training
7. Competitive wages and benefits
8. High expectations

Chapters 4 through 11 will provide an overview of each element. It is important to note that few people will find any fault with the elements themselves. Companies espouse these elements as values on a frequent basis. But far too often, companies' processes, policies, and management behavior either do not demonstrate these values or are in direct contradiction to them.

HPWP Group, to which the authors belong, is a tightly knit group of practitioners who've held executive and management positions within medium and large companies. HPWP Group has been partnering with companies for decades to implement this philosophy and management system that works. Leaders who have been exposed to this approach frequently comment, "This is common sense; why isn't every company doing this?" We'll answer that question in the upcoming chapters.

In the following section, the eight elements will be examined in more detail. We will compare and contrast traditional management styles and procedures with the engaging and collaborative mindset of high-performance leadership.

Our HPWP Group has partnered with leaders throughout a wide range of industries, helping them implement and grow a culture of commitment. Several examples from our HPWP experiences are included throughout the book to demonstrate the impact and value of this nontraditional approach. We'll also insert what we've come to call "Kenisms"—shorthand pieces of wisdom that define an important mindset, or an important action to take.

At the beginning of each chapter, you will be introduced to a leader who is experiencing an issue or crisis relating to that high-performance element. Following the chapter's discussion of that element, you will see how the leaders in the scenarios challenge themselves to pursue a more nontraditional, people-focused approach to working through the conflict. In doing so, they achieve levels of commitment and performance they had previously thought were unattainable.

THE HIGH PERFORMANCE CULTURE

CHAPTER **4**
Lead With Positive Assumptions

The New Line

Jeff slumped down in his chair and stared at his phone. He was going to have to call his son and tell him he would miss another baseball game. As he reached for the phone, his boss, Jason, walked in. Three months ago, Jason had set the deadline for completing the new production line installation. It was now five weeks away.

"I wanted to let you know as soon as I could," Jason said. "That big Hartford order came through. We need to have that line up in two weeks." Jason was the operations manager at Wilson Plastics, a midsize manufacturer of plastic toys. Jeff was the plant manager.

"Two weeks?" Jeff exclaimed. "I wasn't sure we could make the original schedule." Jason and Jeff had worked together for eight years, and Jeff was familiar with project schedules being shortened.

"I know," Jason said as he headed for the door. "But we have to make this happen."

A bit shell-shocked after Jason's announcement, Jeff sat a few minutes before giving us a call. Here at HPWP Group, as soon as Bob answered the phone, he recognized Jeff's voice. We had been working with Wilson Plastics for six months, helping them implement processes that would create a higher-performing work environment.

Jeff sounded exhausted as he told Bob what was happening. Bob said he'd meet with him first thing the next day.

"Late night?" Bob asked as he entered Jeff's office.

"That's putting it mildly," Jeff groaned. "I don't know how we'll make this new deadline. I'm just not sure the crew is up to it."

Bob looked at the whiteboard on the wall near Jeff's desk. "Are those your employees?"

Jeff nodded.

"So, what's the problem?"

"Well, Mary and Sal always need to leave right at 4:00. Butch and Phil and Doug just don't have the background or desire to offer more than they already do. Bud and Renee barely do enough to keep their jobs."

"And the rest?" Bob asked.

Jeff pointed at the first name and began to go down the list. "No passion. No desire. Doesn't care about the company. Doesn't want to make decisions. Avoids any kind of responsibili—"

Bob interrupted him, pointing. "What about these two?"

"She's lazy, and he's lazier." Jeff deadpanned. "Sometimes I wish I could just start with an entirely new group. If I had people who were really enthusiastic and committed to getting this line installed, we might be able to get somewhere."

Bob went on. "How much have you told your team about the project—about the new production line?"

Jeff's frustration was growing. "I've told them what they need to know. But most of them don't want to know much. And that's not the way we've done things around here. Look, they're production workers. They're not supposed to be doing my job."

Bob looked at Jeff. "It sounds like you don't think they're really capable. Why is that?"

Jeff is a perfect example of how negative assumptions about coworkers can sabotage both the work environment and the ability to accomplish what we hope to.

Why is it that we tend to have more negative assumptions about people than positive? Is it because most of what we see and read in the news is negative? Is it because some of us have jobs that require us to deal with the small part of the population that lies, cheats, and steals? Have we personally had bad experiences when we were duped and now look at most strangers with a jaundiced eye? It could be any of these reasons, and we'll talk more about that in chapter 6. But first, let's talk about the impact our assumptions have on the way leaders behave.

Beliefs Drive Behavior

In the 1950s, Douglas McGregor, a professor at MIT Sloan School of Management, developed a philosophical view of people based on two opposing perceptions about how people behave in the workplace. His studies showed that leaders' underlying assumptions about people drive these approaches. Theory X is a command-and-control management style based on the perception that people have an inherent dislike for work and will avoid it whenever possible; they must be coerced, controlled, directed, or threatened with punishment to get them to achieve objectives. People prefer to be directed, do not want responsibility, and have little or no ambition. Based on these perceptions, a command-and-control style would appear to be the most effective.

But McGregor also offered Theory Y, the opposing belief, that posits for most people, work is as natural as play and rest; people will exercise self-direction if committed to its objectives; creativity, ingenuity, and imagination are widely distributed among the population; and people have potential.

Generally, traditionally managed organizations operate from negative assumptions. Jeff personified this attitude, which seemed to match the overall philosophy of his company ("… that's not how we've done things around here.")

When leaders proceed from negative assumptions, they believe that people, by nature:

- Lack integrity
- Are fundamentally lazy and desire to work as little as possible
- Avoid responsibility
- Are not interested in achievement
- Are incapable of directing their own behavior
- Are indifferent to the organization needs
- Prefer to be directed by others
- Avoid making decisions
- Are not very bright

While no one believes this is true of everyone, experiences with five-percenters often cause management to paint an entire employee group with this broad brush.

Don't the majority of people deserve positive assumptions? When leaders begin with positive assumptions, they believe that people:

- Have integrity
- Work hard toward objectives to which they are committed

- Assume responsibility within the scope of those commitments
- Desire to achieve
- Are capable of directing their own behavior
- Want the organization to succeed
- Are not passive or submissive
- Will make decisions within the scope of their commitments
- Are bright

Assumptions about People Drive Our Behavior

There's a marked difference between behavior and attitude. Judging someone's attitude is a subjective determination. Yet if we believe someone has a bad attitude, we are usually able to describe that in terms of behaviors: doesn't smile, states what won't work versus what can work, ignores requests for help, bad-mouths the company to others, etc.

Strike the word *attitude* from your vocabulary when you are describing others. Instead, describe the *behaviors* that led you to reach your conclusion regarding someone's attitude. It's also important to describe behaviors when talking about such concepts as trust. What behaviors demonstrate trust?

On four separate sheets of paper with the labels below, make a few notes to describe what *behaviors* demonstrate the assumptions management and employees may have about each other, both positive and negative.

Start with management's negative assumptions about employees. In the second box describe employee behaviors that reflect negative assumptions and perceptions they may have about management.

Management: Negative Behaviors	Employees: Negative Behaviors
Negative Behavior	Negative Behavior
Negative Behavior	Negative Behavior
Negative Behavior	Negative Behavior
Negative Behavior	Negative Behavior
Negative Behavior	Negative Behavior
Negative Behavior	Negative Behavior
Negative Behavior	Negative Behavior

Next, make a few notes in the first box below to describe what *behaviors* management exhibits that demonstrate *positive assumptions* about employees. Finish by describing in the second box *behaviors* employees would exhibit if they have positive assumptions and perceptions about management.

Management: Positive Behaviors	Employees: Positive Behaviors
Positive Behavior	Positive Behavior
Positive Behavior	Positive Behavior
Positive Behavior	Positive Behavior
Positive Behavior	Positive Behavior
Positive Behavior	Positive Behavior
Positive Behavior	Positive Behavior
Positive Behavior	Positive Behavior

Your lists probably contain many of the behaviors below, which are common in many workplaces.

Management: Negative Behaviors	Employees: Negative Behaviors
Micromanage	Talk badly about the company
Create and enforce lots of rules	Hide mistakes
Lock stuff up	Do the minimum
Minimize responsibility	Don't come to work
Talk down to employees	Quit
Restrict access	Say, "It's not my job"
Look for who to blame	Come in late
Ignore them	Display low energy, no passion
Don't ask for input or ideas	Don't volunteer
Withhold information	Resist change
Have timeclocks for hourly workers	Gossip
Communicate low expectations	Show no accountability

Look at the **Management: Negative Behaviors** list here and the one you created. When employees see and feel these behaviors, how do you suppose they will react? They will display the behaviors you have listed under **Employee: Negative Behaviors**. But it doesn't just stop there.

Now, what happens when management sees these behaviors in employees? Because management had negative assumptions from the start, they see their assumptions have now been *proven*. They are now facts, and management will display even more of the behaviors in the first list. The more they practice these negative behaviors, the stronger the negative reaction from the employees. This continues in a downward spiral of negative behaviors that has become prevalent in traditional work environments.

Now let's look at it from the other perspective. Look at **Management: Positive Behaviors** and **Employees: Positive Behaviors**.

Management: Positive Behaviors	Employees: Positive Behaviors
Challenge people	Brag about the company
Celebrate successes	Recruit others
Eliminate silly behavior rules	Give 110 percent
Make tools and supplies easily accessible	Offer ideas
Broaden all jobs—expand responsibility	Solve problems
Share information	Train new employees
Look for the cause of a problem, not who's guilty	Support change
Challenge thinking and creativity	Are loyal/don't leave
Lots of two-way communication	Welcome visitors/customers
Brag about employee accomplishments	Volunteer for extra projects
Communicate high expectations	Look for opportunities to engage

When leadership embraces the behaviors shown in your positive assumptions list, what reaction will that elicit in the employees? You will see employee actions and conduct in line with those in the corresponding list. And when leadership sees that level of performance, they will enthusiastically exhibit more of the positive behaviors that they originally assumed. And this spiral goes in the direction most leaders want their spirals to go—up.

Assumptions versus Facts

It's not a negative assumption if experience has demonstrated that a failure to meet expectations has happened before, consistently, on the part of the same person or group. There's still a need for problem solving, but at least you know the problem doesn't lie in part with you.

The Creation of Silos

Have you ever been frustrated when another work group, department, shift, or division hasn't delivered as planned and that has negatively impacted you or your team's performance? What assumptions did you make about the other group's failure to meet your expectations? Did you and others find yourself thinking poorly of the other team in general? This is just one of several ways silos develop, but negative assumptions further this dysfunctional organization factor.

Having worked with many large corporations, it's become clear that some of the fiercest and most bitter competition exists under the same roof. Whether it's operations versus sales, operations versus maintenance, quality versus production, or Human Resources versus everybody, boundaries are drawn, blame is cast, and decisions are rationalized.

Assumptions drive our behavior. If one group has positive assumptions about another, the response to a failed action would logically be to find out what happened and assist in solving the problem. However, if the same thing happens and one group has negative assumptions about the other, the response is often to share frustrations with those on the same team and document the other group's failure. Not only does problem-solving not occur, but walls between the groups become stronger.

Silos can also be created by incompatible objectives, competing bonuses, and management territorialism. These causes may be more difficult to overcome. Challenging ourselves and others to have positive assumptions, however, is an easy organizational habit to develop. It drives cross-functional problem-solving and creates a significant decrease in non-value-added conflict.

Not the Chicken or the Egg

A leader's job is to create a working environment that promotes passion, loyalty, maximum effort, and pride in the company. This cannot be accomplished without first operating based on positive assumptions. When companies see waste, poor quality, compliance instead of commitment, strong resistance to change, people doing the minimum, turnover, and absenteeism, this reflects management beliefs and behaviors.

In the book *Maverick,* visionary leader Ricardo Semler describes how his family's traditional company transformed into one that defied virtually all closely held standard management practices.[1] His career at Semler has been covered by the news media worldwide. Below is an excerpt from a 1989 *Harvard Business Review* article that is as relevant today as it was then.

"We hire adults, and then we treat them like adults. Think about that. Outside the factory, workers are men and women who elect governments, serve in the army, lead community projects, raise and educate family, and make decisions every day about the future. Friends solicit their advice. Salespeople court them. Children and grandchildren look up to them for their wisdom and experience. But the moment they walk into the factory, the company transforms them into adolescents."[2]

Most people who work in organizations are good people who own homes, raise children, coach children's sports teams, and contribute to their churches and communities. Why should they be treated as anything less than responsible adults?

Operating from positive assumptions drives people to problem-solve versus blame. It relieves anger and frustration, promotes teamwork,

---

[1] Semler, Ricardo. *Maverick!: The Success behind the World's Most Unusual Workplace.* London : Arrow, 1994.
[2] Semler, Ricardo. "Managing Without Managers." *Harvard Business Review.* August 01, 2014. https://hbr.org/1989/09/managing-without-managers.

results in solutions, and promotes trust and respect. It eliminates non-value-added, time-consuming CYA activities and fosters commitment versus compliance—all critical organizational behaviors for high performance. And the best part of it is that it costs nothing and can be entirely controlled by leaders. As Jeff experienced in the opening story, negative assumptions elicit stress and become an obstacle to higher performance.

The New Line, Part Two

Jeff had no answer when Bob asked why he assumed his employees weren't capable.

"Look, let's start here," Bob continued. "Who are three of your best employees?"

Jeff thought for a moment. "Probably Tim, Dan, and Angie."

Bob suggested that Jeff get Tim and Dan and Angie together that afternoon. Jeff would describe the project to them and tell them about the concerns that he had and what he was struggling with. He would emphasize how critical it was that the project be completed in two weeks, and he would challenge them to get others involved.

"But if I do that," Jeff said, "it will look like they have to figure this out, like I'm having them do my job. And even if they don't think that, my boss will."

"Let's say that's true," Bob said. "Isn't he concerned about getting this up and running on time, and seeing that his employees are all doing their best? So, if that happens and you're their leader, won't he think you're doing a *good* job?"

Jeff thought about that, and then despite his concerns, agreed to give the approach a try.

The next morning, Bob asked Jeff about the meeting. "It wasn't what I expected," Jeff said. He went on to describe the input he'd received when he laid out the blueprints. Dan had worked through a similar installation at his previous job six years ago, and Angie used to install conveyor systems. The employees continued to talk and to brainstorm, and they volunteered to stay late or work weekends to get the project completed on time. Tim was going to get four other employees together to create an action team to produce a day-by-day schedule to keep the accelerated project on track.

"But now I just need to take all of this...stuff," he looked around his office, "and put my new plan together and get this going."

"What about them? What about your people?" Bob asked.

"What do you mean? You wanted me to start with the assumption that they cared, and I did. I've got their ideas, and now I need to move forward."

Bob suggested to Jeff that he should continue to talk with them, involve them in the project, and challenge them. The meeting was evidence that they were capable and wanted to contribute. Jeff disagreed and again expressed his thoughts that it would appear he wasn't doing his job or didn't know how.

Bob continued to challenge Jeff. "What will be the effect on your team when they see that you don't want them involved in completing this project when you have those negative assumptions? Will they be more or less likely to showcase their abilities?"

"I don't know," Jeff said, searching for an answer. "I hope it shows them that I know what I'm doing. I mean, I'm using some of their ideas." He paused. "But I can see the message that would send, especially to the rest of the team."

The next day Jeff called another meeting with the entire group. He had clearly thought about Bob's question and gave the team time to discuss ideas. He recorded their thoughts and suggestions on flipcharts. Soon, one of the packaging operators, Blaine, spoke up. "We still have to reconfigure the access from the new line to the loading bay." The team was silent for a few seconds. Jeff nodded. "I don't think I had thought much about that. I've just been focusing on getting the line going. Can I get three volunteers to get together after this meeting to start laying out the details for that?" The meeting continued for another forty-five minutes. Afterward, Jeff made his way back to his office, flipcharts in hand. "I think we're going to make it," he said quietly to himself.

That Friday afternoon, Bob got a call from Jeff. They had finished the job, and Jeff was excited and relieved. They still had to fix a processor software glitch and recalibrate one of the packaging units, but nothing that would keep production from starting on the new line. And he was amazed at the response he got from his people. "Once Tim and Dan and Angie got behind it, others started to help out too. I didn't know that they cared so much about this place, and about helping me. They're certainly more than just production workers." Jeff also mentioned that his boss, Jason, was very pleased with his hard work and effort to meet the deadline. "I told him it wasn't me. It was the entire team. He said he agreed, but he was sure I had something to do with that."

Once Jeff shifted his assumptions about his team— started seeing them as conscientious and capable people who cared about the company and who were doing their best—and treated them accordingly based on that knowledge, the outcomes were startling. Not only was the production line up and running on time, but Jeff's relationships with his employees, and their feelings of satisfaction with their own jobs, were also transformed.

Even the setbacks they encountered were solved by the team in a spirit of cooperation rather than blame. And Jeff's stress level—as well as his standing with his own boss—was better than he thought possible.

Four months later, Bob stopped by to see Jeff. He wasn't in his office, so Bob asked Kerry, a production team member working nearby, if he had seen Jeff. Kerry said he had left to get to his son's baseball game.

"He took off early?" Bob asked, a little surprised.

"Yeah, he's been making it to most of Zach's games lately. There are enough of us here to cover until he gets back."

"Gets back?" Bob asked.

"Yeah, he's coming back in later. We had another big order come in just this morning, and we all have to put our heads together to figure out how to get it done."

CHAPTER **5**
Identify and Eliminate Negatives

A Death in the Family

Claire, the floor manager at the customer call center for Placker Distributing, had just returned from lunch Monday. As she was walking down the hall, she noticed someone sitting in her office. The person was looking down, and she couldn't tell who it was.

When she walked in, Conner raised his head and looked at her as he wiped his eyes.

"What's wrong?" she asked as she sat down next to him. Conner was one of the newer customer support specialists and had been with the company for about two weeks.

"I just got a call that my father passed away this morning," he said. "It was pretty sudden, and I need to get back to Seattle. I've got stuff I'll need to help my mom with; you know, arrangements and everything."

"I'm so sorry," Claire said. "What can I do for you?"

"Well, I guess I need to know if I can be gone this week. I'd like to leave this afternoon."

"Absolutely. We'll be able to cover for you," Claire said.

Conner then asked about bereavement leave. Having been there for less than thirty days, he hadn't yet accrued full benefits. When Claire checked the policy manual, she told him that the bereavement leave designated for a parent was three days but, due to his short tenure, he was not eligible for any paid bereavement leave.

"Can I take some vacation time?" he asked.

"Well, you haven't accrued any of that yet either," Claire said. "I can give you the week off, but it will have to be unpaid."

Conner said he understood and slowly got up to leave.

"I'm really sorry," Claire said. "I wish there was more I could do."

As she sat at her desk, something didn't feel right. She thought back to the interview she'd had with Conner just a few weeks ago. He was such an excellent fit for her group, and she knew then he would be a valued addition to the team. She contemplated the impact of the bereavement policy. Why should he, or anyone, need to worry about pay and benefits at a time like this? She knew that if she had to be absent for a similar situation, there would be no issue with her taking the time she needed. Why should the two situations be any different?

In a high-performance work environment, a negative is not something someone simply doesn't like. Negatives have a very specific definition, and that is:

*Anything that **minimizes** versus **maximizes** a person's feeling of **value** to the organization.*

No one wants to feel that they are not valued, or worse yet, feel devalued. Yet many traditional organizations, often unintentionally, have policies and practices that minimize versus maximize a person's feeling of value to the company.

Negatives in the workplace show up in four different ways:

- Management behavior and practices based on negative assumptions about people
- Policies created to protect the organization from the five-percenters but enforced equally to all
- Policies, practices, or behaviors that cause one group of people to feel like second class citizens
- Greater management attention and investment in facilities and equipment versus human comfort and development

Many negatives that exist in companies have been there for so long they seem to go unnoticed—even by the people who should feel less valued. Still, managers lament that employees don't take ownership and accountability, people aren't motivated, and there's a lack of passion and loyalty. While people may not consciously think or verbally state that they feel less valued, it is reflected in how committed they feel to the company.

Leaders have unintentionally created an environment in which a person's value as a unique and contributing human being has been seriously damaged through the existence of the above four negatives.

Management Behavior Based on Negative Assumptions

The previous chapter described how negative assumptions affect people's behavior. Even with the best of intentions, leaders who micromanage are communicating a lack of confidence in the employee to be thorough, accurate, and timely. When the company is willing to accept mediocrity in its workforce, it sends the message that this is the best that it can expect. When supervisors don't actively encourage people to raise new ideas for improvement or to participate in solving problems, people recognize that their brainpower is not highly regarded.

In contrast, high-performance companies treat everyone in the workforce with the same level of respect. Self-managed and highly involved organizations demonstrate their positive assumptions about people by challenging them, celebrating successes, broadening job responsibilities, investing in training, and encouraging teams to take on many of the responsibilities currently held by front-line supervisors, including problem-solving and decision-making.

This type of workplace respect was demonstrated in an organization our HPWP Group worked with a few years ago. It was a beverage company that made deliveries seven days a week. Weekend scheduling was often problematic. It was harder to find people who wanted to work the schedule created by the managers. In addition, weekends rarely went uninterrupted for management due to one problem or another. Having had exposure to the HPWP approach to leadership, Alex, the route manager, decided he would put the drivers in touch with each other, and they could plan the weekend routes themselves.

He expected his phone to ring all weekend with problems but did not receive a single call. Upon returning to work Monday, he learned that all had gone smoothly and there hadn't been the usual complaints about the schedule from his drivers. In fact, he felt a new sense of camaraderie. It hit him that positive assumptions had to start with him. When he demonstrated his trust and confidence, his team responded in kind.

In a high-performance environment, when someone makes a derogatory comment about another person or department, it is not uncommon for team members to challenge in a friendly way: "Is that a negative assumption?"

Policies Created to Catch the 5 Percent

Fear can be an intense motivator. Fear of litigation has driven many companies, especially the larger ones, to institutionalize volumes of insulting and dehumanizing policies. Add to that progressive discipline policies with the strong admonition that everyone must be treated the same, and organizations have created another major way to make people feel less valued.

An unhealthy portion of management's time is spent dealing with the bad apples. In attempting to catch them, or trying to stop them, organizations create longs lists of conduct rules—let's call them "Thou Shalt Not" rules. Often, they're even prioritized by the seriousness of the infraction, accompanied by appropriate discipline. One company actually displayed a large matrix that showed what type of punishment accompanied what infraction.

For the ninety-five-percenters, this is insulting and unnecessary. For the five-percenters, it's a game plan.

In addition to "Thou Shalt Not" rules, several other standard policies further devalue and insult competent and well-intentioned adults.

Traditional Policies

- **Attendance policies** are transformed into point systems, allowing a mathematical means for five-percenters to manipulate the system. Little problem-solving, or even communication, happens, and the talented abusers at one client we worked with had figured out how to take as many as twenty-two days or more off in a year and still have a job.

- **Bereavement policies**, as presented in the opening story, are overstructured, overcomplicated, and heartless. In these policies, the number of days an employee is normally allowed to be off to grieve is three days—but only if it's a blood relative. In-laws often qualify an employee for only one day of leave (the fallacy in determining the time needed for grieving has been emphasized by Ken, who has said that, if his dog dies, he needs two weeks; if his mother-in-law dies, it's fifteen minutes, a cup of coffee, a jig in the hall, and he's back to work). How does the company know how grief-stricken someone should be? What about best friends or the aunt who raised someone? There are no days off to grieve in these cases. And, to really drive home the assumption that people will take advantage of the death of a loved one, many policies require documentation from the funeral home.

- **Probationary periods** are common. One reason for instituting probationary periods is the mistaken belief that it is easier to fire a bad hire more easily within the first ninety days. Leaders need to start by making sure everyone they recruit and hire is someone they expect to be an outstanding person and performer. Isn't that the goal? If it is, then a probationary period communicates a lack of initial trust and value. And who are the people we generally associate with being on probation? Criminals! Here's a fact: every five-percenter can count to ninety. And this is why we refer to these types of policies as their "game plan." On the ninety-first day, the true five-percenter will come shining through.

- The **progressive disciplinary policy** is a mainstay for dealing with policy violators. Five-percenters know how to work this system as well, while most good people are subjected to one-way, often parent-child-style communication, threatened with further disciplinary action, and required to sign documents to acknowledge they have been disciplined. Again, no one knows the rules (and how to get around them) better than the five-percenter.

These policies, created for the five-percenters, are applied to the majority of good people as well. When companies let policy stand in the way of good judgment, they communicate that an employee is just a number and that years of good service mean little. So, what should companies do instead?

Commonsense Replacements (for Traditional Policies)

Years ago, Ken simplified all the "Thou Shalt Not" rules into one simple code of conduct:

Everyone is expected to act in the best interest of the company and their fellow employees.

It's hard to identify a conduct or performance issue that wouldn't be covered by this standard.

- Point systems (another strategy in the five-percenter's playbook) and ridiculous definitions for attendance are replaced with the simple expectation that leaders expect everyone to be at work, every day, on time.

- Bereavement leave is determined following a discussion with the employee regarding what time is needed. Time and pay are then determined based on whether the time off seems necessary and pay seems reasonable. And employees often offer their own solutions.

- There is no discipline system in a high-performance workplace. Discipline in this sense carries a punishment, and punishment doesn't make people better. It makes them minimally compliant. Verbal warnings, written warnings, and suspensions are not effective in solving performance issues. Probing for the cause of an undesired action or behavior, and expecting the employee to be *responsive* and *responsible* for resolving it, results in faster and more positive outcomes. If an employee doesn't choose to solve their issue, then they have chosen not to work for the company. Not only is this approach more efficient, fairer, and more respectful, it's also legally more defensible.

- There is no probationary period. It is expected that the decision to hire and promote people is one that requires careful consideration up front. To do less conveys a lack of confidence and trust. Companies using probationary periods justify them by saying that it's a two-way street—an opportunity for the employee to determine if the position is the right fit as well. But the selection process should maximize opportunities for both parties to make this important decision.

Policies and Practices that Create Second-Class Status

When one group of people is treated better than another group that has less responsibility, the second group is repeatedly reminded of its lesser value through subtle practices and visible symbols. In most industries, many of the policies just discussed don't apply to managers, salaried employees, or office staff. The disparity may not be clearly stated in the policy manual, but everyone understands that it is the reality. (How many managers are hired with a designated probationary period, or are expected to produce a doctor's note to get paid?)

Visible signs of status differences can be seen in reserved parking, free coffee and water in the office but not in the plant, restricted access to certain areas of the building, and separate eating and break rooms.

Many years ago, a highly traditional aerospace company was having the executive dining room remodeled. To accommodate the company directors and vice presidents, a temporary partition had been raised in the general cafeteria. While the cafeteria was always noisy, with hundreds of hungry people cycling through, this day it was quiet. None of the employees spoke as they stood in line with their trays, plastic utensils, and choice of hotdogs, cold sandwiches, or meatloaf. Coming from the other side of the partition they could hear the clinking of crystal, smell the aroma of steak flambé and glazed salmon, and hear the murmuring of servers asking if the diners would prefer steak or seafood.

That day everyone in the general cafeteria felt less important and less valued. This was a company that always touted people as its most important asset. The executive dining room was only one demonstration of how little those words really meant.

With several thousand employees in the facility, parking was often far away, but job status dictated how close someone could park to the plant. Every morning, managers and executives drove through the gate to their reserved parking spots. As they did, they passed a lot of long-time employees hiking in from the north forty, then waiting at the guard gate because they were denied entrance until the start of their shift. It was particularly demoralizing one Friday when two hundred people were exiting the main gate on their way home to tell their families that their jobs had been eliminated as a cost-cutting measure. As they left, they had a direct view of the scaffolding around the executive offices that were being remodeled to provide larger windows.

Symbols of second-class status are widespread and prevalent in our workplaces today. This is just one kind of negative that prevents people from feeling passion and loyalty for their companies.

Popular programs in many organizations today can easily become negatives. One such common program is Employee of the Month. With good intentions to create more visible, positive recognition, many companies choose an individual for this recognition. His or her picture is taken, framed, and hung on a wall. The employee may even get a reserved parking space for that month. Excellent; we have a winner. And also a whole lot of losers who feel less valued.

Ken is a joyous troublemaker and regularly highlights well-intentioned, but misguided programs and policies. On a recent visit to the printing area of an office supply store, Ken saw an eight-by-ten framed picture of a young woman showcasing her as the employee of the month. Another associate politely asked if she could help us. Ken looked at her, looked at the picture, then looked at her again and asked if he could work with the employee of the month because he was only interested in the best service. Quickly catching on, the associate said, "Don't worry, I was employee of the month last time. We all get named sooner or later."

Another way well-intentioned leaders try to recognize good performance is the perfect attendance award. This was created to *incent* people to come to work every day. In a high-performance environment, it's our *expectation* that people come to work every day. Assuming everyone understands this expectation and intends to honor it, perfect attendance awards rely on good luck and have nothing to do with the employee's performance or quality of work. It means that a person was fortunate to not have any major illnesses, sick children, traffic accidents, home fires, floods, etc. Additionally, it promotes people coming to work when they are sick and should be staying at home, so they don't make *others* sick.

Greater Attention to Equipment and Facilities versus People

There are five ways in which companies today unintentionally communicate less value for people than facilities and equipment.

1. **Machines are calibrated to improve maximum function.**
    But do we invest the same time and dollars in maximizing
    the capacity of our workforce? Gallup reports that only 31.5
    percent of U.S. workers are actively engaged while at work.[3]
    If only one-third of our machines were functioning at maximum
    capacity, they'd be retooled or replaced. Yet companies are only
    tapping the surface of their human assets' capacity. Investing
    in and engaging people offers almost unlimited opportunity in
    terms of quality, innovation, and efficiency.

2. **Machines are showcased.** Plant tours are usually led by
    managers who point out each piece of high-value equipment
    along the way—what it can do and how fast it can do it. The
    operator frequently stands back, out of the way. In high-
    performing plants, tours showcase the operator at each stop
    by asking him to explain his role in the process, and how the
    equipment works and enhances the output.

3. **Machines draw more investment capital.** One company's
    division leader proudly described that the new company
    headquarters had cost millions of dollars and had been paid
    for in cash. When asked how team members were trained and
    developed, the division leader promptly cited company policy:
    "Any team member training must take place after hours on
    non-company time." She then added that, at this point, the
    company was also unable to provide any company-sponsored
    training or reimbursement for team member development.

---

[3] Gallup, Inc. "State of the American Workplace." Gallup.com. February 15, 2017. http://news.gallup.
com/reports/178514/state-americanworkplace.aspx.

4. **Machines are fixed when they break.** Companies go to great lengths to repair, salvage, or save equipment. The cost of bringing a broken machine back online through further investment seems to be easily accepted. Yet, when an employee's performance requires attention and repair, we quickly move to discipline and documentation with the intent that the employee will fix himself or herself (after being warned) or will eventually be terminated.

5. **There are often stark differences in the appearance of corporate lobbies and restrooms when compared to employee break rooms.** This does not mean companies must have a one-to-one ratio of facilities and equipment to people, but they must consider the size of this disparity and what message it's sending.

It's astonishing to see all the ways companies can minimize a person's sense of value to the company, and this is critical for leaders to understand. The good news is that so many of these negatives are easy to fix. Look at your organization with a fresh set of eyes. Find the negatives and take every action possible to eliminate them. If people do not feel valued, it is *irrational* for leaders to expect them to have high levels of passion and dedication to the company. Ken has always asserted that the single, most powerful way to build motivation and loyalty in people is by strengthening the feeling of value that they bring to the organization. That is what leaders do.

A Death in the Family, Part Two

Claire picked up her phone and called Conner's station. She nervously tapped her pencil waiting for an answer. Finally, she put the phone down and headed toward the customer service area. Not seeing Conner, she asked a nearby customer service representative if she knew where he might be. She said he had just left and he said he would be back next week. She began to look up his number on her phone and hurried toward the elevator.

Conner answered her call as he was getting in his car. Claire asked him to meet her in the lobby.

"Conner, I'm glad I caught you. Look, I got to thinking about this. You're going to have a lot on your mind this week, and probably for some time to come. I don't want you to have to worry about money or your job or your work getting done. I'm going to make sure you get paid for this week. You're a valued employee, and I want to make sure you know that."

Conner looked at Claire and struggled to find the right words. "Thanks," he finally said. "That really means a lot."

As Claire got onto the elevator to head back to her office, she wondered if she had done the right thing.

As the door opened, she saw Marilyn, the human resources manager, in the hall.

"Do you have a minute?" Claire asked as she walked off the elevator.

"Sure," Marilyn said. They walked in to Claire's office and sat down.

Claire explained Conner's situation to Marilyn and told her that she wanted to pay him for his time off. Marilyn expressed several concerns. What about the next person who needed bereavement leave? What if someone had another kind of emergency that they needed to attend to? If the company deviated from policy, wouldn't it have to bend the rules for everyone?

"I understand your concerns," Claire said. "But why should he be penalized by losing a week's pay just because he's only been here a short time? I just don't think there should be any difference in how we treat a situation like this whether it's a short-term or long-term employee."

Because Claire had already told Conner she would pay him, Marilyn agreed. "But just for this time. We need to have more discussion about this with the executive group before we deviate from the policy again."

When Conner returned to work the following Monday, he went directly to Claire's office. She looked up as he stepped into the doorway.

Claire looked up and smiled. "How are you?"

"Good," he replied. "It was tough, but we made it through the week." Then Conner gave a half-smile. "Thanks again for breaking the rules and paying me for the week. It was good to not have to worry about that."

"Well, as far as rules, that is one that the company will be discussing. I want to talk more about it with the leadership group, but I feel like it's the right thing to do. If someone needs time off, they need time off."

"Sounds good. And thanks again." Conner said.

As he turned to leave, Claire spoke up. "I wanted to thank you too, Conner. Samantha told me that you called in twice Thursday and once Friday to see how everything was going." Connor shrugged and nodded. Claire smiled. "We're glad you're back."

CHAPTER **6**
Build Trust and Mutual Respect

The Tool Room

Jack had filled the role of project superintendent for seventeen years with Beckett Construction. He was highly regarded in the field and had a reputation for building great crews that worked exceptionally well together. About nine months before current events, he had developed problems with his back, and it was determined that he would no longer be able to perform job site work. Hal, the current yard and equipment manager, was preparing to retire and company leadership knew that Jack would be a great asset in filling that role. When he was offered the position, he quickly accepted and looked forward to the new challenges it would bring.

Jack knew most of the current processes at the yard facility, having dealt with Hal and his people daily during his tenure as a superintendent. On his first day at the new job, as he was getting acclimated to his role, one of the things he noticed was that the tool room wasn't locked. It had a deadbolt lock on the door that, according to one of the yard employees, had been broken for years. Jack immediately went to the hardware store and purchased a new deadbolt, along with an additional clasp and padlock. He stayed after closing time that afternoon to install them.

The next morning, he was at his desk reviewing purchase orders and safety manuals when Rick, the assistant yard manager, stepped into his doorway. Rick was the senior person in the yard, and he and Jack had known each other for years.

"Hey, great to see you in here Jack. I see the tool room is locked," Rick said with an inquisitive tone.

"Yeah," Jack said, looking up. "I did that last night. We've got a lot of high-dollar stuff in there. I just want to make sure none of it walks off."

Rick asked for the key and returned in a few minutes. "Here you go," he said as he handed it back to Jack. As the week went on, Jack found himself handing the key over at some point to most everyone who worked in the yard. They would get what they needed, then promptly bring the key back to him.

Thursday afternoon, Rick made his fourth stop at Jack's office to get the key. As Jack handed it over, Rick asked him, "Just curious, Jack. Why do you think we need the tool room locked?"

"Well," Jack grinned as he looked up. "I've been around too many years. You leave something unlocked for even a little while and it will disappear. I can't tell you how much stuff we've lost on job sites."

"Sure. But there, you're working with people you don't know—other contractors. We're the only ones here during the day," Rick replied.

"Yeah, but like I said before, expensive tools are tempting and it's too easy for someone to take something," Jack said.

"Well, I've worked with this group a long time, Jack, and none of them would do that. I think doing this makes it look like you think otherwise."

Jack leaned back in his chair and thought for a moment about what Rick had said, then shrugged his shoulders. "They'll get used to it," he said. "In a couple of weeks, they won't think anything about it."

During the next week, Jack started keeping a spare key with him to avoid going back to his office to retrieve it when someone asked for it. And he continued to think about what Rick had said. Jack knew the people who worked in the yard. There wasn't one of them he couldn't trust. Would any of them really steal something? But was that trust worth the risk of leaving thousands of dollars' worth of equipment unprotected?

"Trust is like the air we breathe. When it is present, nobody really notices. But when it's absent, everybody notices." This quote by Warren Buffet at once captures the invisible concept and palpable impact of trust.

As humans, we recognize the importance of trust. It's the foundation for family and relationships. Like positive assumptions, trust drives behavior. When there's trust, people become more expansive—frank, honest, and spontaneous. There's more acceptance of others' attitudes, feelings, and differences. Communication becomes clearer. People are more willing to risk conflict.

And these behaviors drive a high-performance organization.

Recognizing a Trust Organization

We're assuming every organization would like to be recognized as a trusting workplace. And there are probably many definitions. Here are some visible signs that a workplace has a high level of trust and respect, and the resulting high performance.

- If the company has multiple shifts, it's hard to tell when the shifts change. People come and go at different times, taking time to coordinate with coworkers on a previous shift.

- There are no time clocks. All employees, whether exempt or nonexempt, are paid a salary. If overtime is needed, employees are responsible for entering this into the payroll or timekeeping system.

- Everyone has a key or key card that opens every door.

- Supply cabinets, lockers, tool and equipment storage areas are unlocked.

- The security of the facility is entrusted to the employees who work there, and they protect it as they would their home.

Creating a trusting environment is important to everyone reading this book. But how can you get started when there are five-percenters in the organization?

Tolerance for Risk

It's important to assess tolerance for risk—yours and that of the organization. Leaders face different kinds of risks every day. If there is theft or vandalism in an organization, an immediate response may be to mitigate future incidents by locking up valuable equipment and supplies, installing internal cameras, and checking bags as people enter and exit the property. While this may prevent theft in the future, however, these actions also communicate a lack of trust in the majority of trustworthy people. In addition, tools, supplies, and information are often needed to continue a work process, but when they are locked up or information is closely held, this results in a disruption to workflow.

Leaders are paid to use good judgment. This includes protecting company property from vandalism and theft, assuring performance goals and expectations are met, and being fiscally responsible. But the five-percenters jeopardize a leader's credibility and have caused management to enact policy and security measures to protect the company as well as their own individual reputation.

Quickly answer this question about yourself: Do you need people to earn your trust, or are you someone who automatically trusts until that trust is betrayed?

There is no right or wrong answer.

An orientation to trust or not to trust starts with someone's life experience. People who grow up in a city where there is higher crime wisely lock their doors. Professionals in law enforcement often find it hard to trust because they are dealing with the small percent of the population who lie, cheat, and steal. When life experience results in negative consequences, the tendency is to be guarded and operate on the premise that trust must be earned.

The reverse is true as well, and this is important to understand as it applies to creating an environment of trust. In this case, trust is assumed unless there is cause to mistrust. Establishing a trusting culture must start with leadership. And for leaders to feel comfortable in demonstrating trust, a couple of things need to happen first.

1. **Hire for Trust as an Attribute**

    Many companies say that hiring and promoting the best people is job number one, but often there are flaws in this system. In practice, technical knowledge and experience trumps character, as evidenced by interviews that favor the former and frequently don't include behaviorally-based interview questions that can define hidden personal attributes, a lack of in-depth reference checking, and failure to seriously consider feedback from those on the interview team who have real reservations about a candidate.

2. **Communicate Trust as a Value**

    High-performance companies place such a high value on trust, they have the same kind of *zero-tolerance policy* for betraying trust as most companies have for working under the influence of drugs or alcohol. It starts with communicating the clear expectation that any violation of trust, no matter how small or large, is unacceptable. Once this expectation is very clear, anyone who violates trust loses his or her job.

One high-performance company had a long-term employee, Stan, who had worked there for fifteen years and was well-known and well-liked by management and owners. One day, a fellow employee observed him taking a ream of paper from the company supply cabinet to his car. The employee asked Stan what he was doing. He responded, "Let's just say you didn't see this." For team members in a high-performance environment, reporting this type of incident is expected. When asked about the incident by his manager, Stan said he couldn't explain why he had done it. (This company would have given him the paper if he had simply asked for and needed it.) But by taking it and trying to cover it up with his coworker, Stan violated trust. Management was visibly upset the day he was terminated, but there was no outcry from fellow team members as might have been expected. It's now believed they had had some prior suspicions, but this was the first time a violation of this sort had come to light.

A ream of paper. Fifteen years of service. Didn't he deserve a second chance?

Not in a high-performance workplace. As soon as people start to muddy the water with "but it was just a little white lie," or, "it wasn't that big of a deal," there is no longer zero-tolerance. A zero-tolerance policy creates a workplace where everyone can leave personal property unlocked and company tools and equipment openly accessible. It also expands the responsibility for safety and security to every person who works there, and people take it seriously. There is an extremely high level of pride in being part of this type of organization.

Your Trust Orientation

Why is it important for leaders to know their personal trust orientation? When people are trusting, they more naturally have, and operate from, positive assumptions. Chapter 4 clearly showed the positive impact of leading based on positive assumptions.

To use a sports analogy, consider a basketball player talented in offense traded to a team known for defense. That player is now going to have to consciously practice the skills needed to be effective as a defensive player. If a leader has a low trust orientation, does that mean he or she won't be successful in a high-performance work environment? No; it simply means the individual must be more conscious of his or her assumptions and behaviors and consciously commit to practicing trusting behaviors.

An orientation toward certain behaviors can be offset, even when it's strong. Ken has been known to use blue language but has noted that he has never sworn in church. Your orientation can change based on your situation.

Sustaining a Culture of Trust

Even in the most trusting of environments, there may still be instances of theft or deceit. Here's what to do—and more importantly, what not to do—if this happens:

- **Set and communicate the expectation for trust and honesty in clear and exact terms.** Describe the environment and behavior expectations. Ask for the behavior you want.

- **Promote transparency.** There is a difference between hiding information and not sharing information. It's understood that some information is sensitive and proprietary. But hiding information is an act of distrust usually based on negative assumptions regarding how the information will be handled or mishandled by the receivers. It is often less about organizations deliberately withholding information, however, than it is about making transparency a priority—a major factor in creating trust.

- **Take the risk.** No one wants to be fooled or viewed as naïve. But be a leader for the company. Look at how locked doors, tool cribs, and supply cabinets communicate a lack of trust in everyone—not just a few. Lead an initiative to give a key (or key card) to every employee. Stop locking things up.

- **Admit mistakes.** In leadership positions, some mistakes can be extremely visible. Visible or not, when leaders acknowledge they've made a mistake or done something wrong and accept personal accountability, the result is more admiration and trust.

- **Don't install cameras.** If there is a problem of theft, publicly acknowledge the occurrence, then ask for everyone's help in solving the issue while simultaneously reinforcing the company's belief in the integrity of the workforce. When trust is a clearly established value, team members will hold each other accountable.

- **Don't try to trap people or ask them questions about their behaviors, activities, or whereabouts when you already know the answers.** If you are aware of something they have done, address it with them directly.

- **Don't do trunk checks or require employees to carry transparent purses and bags.** If the company believes it must have a guard gate, expect the guard to act as an ambassador for the company and to be welcoming as people come and go—visitors and employees alike. The guard is there to protect both the company *and* the employees.

- **Don't try to categorize the level of a trust violation.** Any action that betrays trust is cause for termination.

It's a leadership responsibility to take risks, use judgment, and operate from positive motives. When companies show trust and respect by eliminating the actions intended to protect themselves, they will see loyalty, dedication, and higher performance from those most critical to the companies' success.

The Tool Room, Part Two

During the next two weeks, Rick continued to talk with Jack about the locks on the tool room, and Jack considered his options. Jack agreed with what Rick had pointed out many times—the group was trustworthy.

One Monday morning, at the end of the weekly planning meeting he held with the team, Jack asked them about their thoughts on leaving the tool room unlocked. As he expected, most were in favor of leaving it open. Jack struggled with that, remembering situations he had experienced on job sites. After more discussion, he told them he would leave it locked, but leave the key on a hook by his office door.

Jill, one of the yard employees, came in one Monday morning to get the key. "Jack, can we just leave the tool room open today? We're going to have to be in and out all day. It would make it a lot easier." Jack said that was fine. The same request was made the next day, and each day for the rest of the week.

The next Monday morning Jack unlocked the tool room as he came in. When Jill came to his office to get the key, Jack looked up. "It's unlocked," he said. "Just make sure to lock it when you go home today."

Jack continued to unlock the room each morning when he came in, and he continued to be anxious about the tools. He wanted his people to know that he trusted their judgment and their honesty, but he didn't want to have to deal with stolen equipment.

One day about a week after Jack began his open-door tool room policy, Rick came in to his office. "Jack, I just wanted to let you know how much more efficient things are around here with the tool room open all the time. It's so much easier to keep things moving. And everyone in the yard appreciates it too. Not just the efficiency, but mostly just knowing that they're trusted."

"Well, thanks, but...," Jack hesitated. "Rick, you know that I've always felt that way about everyone here. I know these people. I have for a long time. I'm more than a little embarrassed that I haven't done a better job of showing it."

CHAPTER 7

Practice Open, Two-Way, Adult-to-Adult Communication

Reply to All

Sal was the director of facilities for WPG, an auto parts manufacturer. He had just put the finishing touches on his email to Mike, one of his direct reports, who was tasked with completing the move-in plan for the company's new headquarters. The email read:

"Two weeks ago, we agreed that you would finish the project plan for the new headquarters move. I DON'T HAVE IT. You clearly don't understand the IMPACT this delay is causing. I expect that plan on my desk by the end of day today!!!!"

He copied five executives. *Good*, he thought. At least this should keep the Mahogany Row guys off my back.

Mike's office was two doors down from Sal, and Mike had a much more negative reaction than Sal had anticipated. What Sal hadn't realized was there had been recent decisions to change the floor plan by the senior group that would delay the move. Having worked hours of overtime with little to no feedback or support from Sal, Mike was ready to blow. Not wanting to have a loud confrontation, and to avoid direct conflict, Mike thought it best to respond in kind.

Clicking the *Reply to All* button, Mike wrote:

"I've been asked to make changes in the floor plans and that has caused the delay. I thought you were informed. If you have a problem with these changes, I suggest you talk to the President."

He promptly hit *Send.*

If asked, almost all leaders would say that one of their key issues is improving communications in the workplace, yet most do not know how to achieve it. While managers and supervisors might think they do not have time to learn all the tactics that are needed for effective workplace communications, there are only three guiding principles they need to know. And these are critical to creating a high trust, high-performance environment.

The Logic Behind Open Communication

The concept of need-to-know information regarding employees is out of date. There is an ever-increasing cry for transparency in all areas of our society today. Transparency builds confidence and trust in leadership. As it relates to the work environment, open communication means that all employees have as much access to information as possible. It's understood that confidential or proprietary information must remain that way. All other information that could have an impact (or even collateral impact) on employees should be shared, or at least made available, to them. This includes financials, plans, production numbers, and growth strategies. In direct terms, transparency means no secrets. Secrets create distrust and stimulate the rumor mill, resulting in nonproductive and even disruptive time.

Why do leaders and organizations withhold information that is not confidential or proprietary? Withholding information is often a result of the negative assumption that employees will not react in a way that management thinks appropriate, especially if the information is perceived as negative. This traditional mindset causes leaders to believe that providing access to information will lead people to gossip, spread rumors, become anxious, or give the information to someone outside the organization. In reality, the opposite is true, and here is why.

Hiding information doesn't change it. In fact, it leads to even more rumors, gossip, panic, and disruption. When facts are presented, the information becomes actionable.

A company was going to close one of its facilities in about six months. Worried that people would start to leave early or even worse, do something harmful, senior management planned to not inform all the plant's employees of the impending closure until two weeks prior. During the preceding six months, most of the employees could see that work had been dramatically decreasing, and anxiety was high that layoffs were imminent. Morale was at rock bottom, tension was heightened, and productivity plummeted. Despite this, respected company advisors encouraged its leaders to make positive assumptions about plant employees, who had proven their loyalty and dedication for many years. The decision was made to provide advance communication instead of waiting. When the information was provided to them, employees started to propose ideas on how to handle the shutdown in a way that best served the company and the employees. As a result of their input, the company experienced a significant increase in productivity and production during the final six months of operation.

Another illustration of the power of open communication occurred when a food-processing company lost a major customer, which meant a significant loss of revenue. Rather than attempting to hide this negative news (which everyone knew about anyway), management led a task force in every functional area to find ways to reduce waste and unnecessary costs. An important exception was that no one would lose his or her job. Over the next three months, the reduction in revenue from losing the contract was offset by identified hard savings of over $1 million—more than the profit from the lost revenue.

As a leader, when you find you are resisting sharing information that could affect employees, check your assumptions. Transparency builds trust, and when people trust, most obstacles are overcome.

Why Two-Way Communication Makes Sense

Start with a simple exercise. In a meeting or training exercise, ask a volunteer to turn his or her back to a group and, given a sheet with the diagram shown on the following page, using *one-way* communication *only*, describe to the group the placement of the five boxes.[4]

---

[4] This exercise is reproduced from *A Handbook of Structured Experiences for Human Relations Training*, Volume I, Revised. J. William Pfeiffer and John E. Jones, Editors San Diego, CA: University Associated, Inc., 1974.

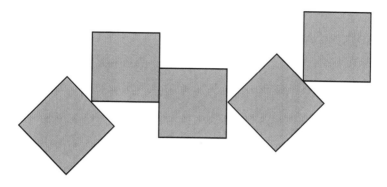

Ask the members of the group to try to draw what the volunteer describes. They can't ask questions or ask for clarification—only the volunteer can talk. After a few minutes, and when the volunteer believes the figure has been described to the best of his or her ability, ask the group about their confidence in the accuracy of their drawings. Members of the group usually say their confidence is very low—"maybe one box?" (Hopefully, they got at least *one* box correct).

Now have the volunteer describe a different set of boxes.

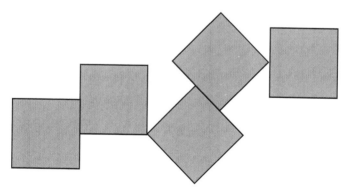

This time, the group still can't see the diagram but can ask questions to help them accurately draw it. After four or five minutes, when the volunteer and the group members feel that they have completed the diagram, ask them about their confidence level. The members will generally say it is very high—"I got all five boxes, I'm sure." When results are compared, the second drawings will be far more accurate.

One-way communication shows up everywhere: emails, memos, texts, standard operating procedures, policy manuals, and productivity reports. The list goes on and on. One-way communication is a great way to disseminate announcements, changes, and information that keeps everyone on the same page. Technology has clearly enhanced our ability to be more broad and efficient in this type of communication.

One-way communication, however, is not the way to resolve conflicts, provide performance feedback, develop plans that require others' commitments, or solve problems creatively—whether in person or via technology.

When one-way communication is used in these situations, it sounds autocratic, sends a message that others' ideas are not valued, and often takes on a parent-child tone. The net result is compliance instead of commitment, malicious obedience, lack of respect and the minimization of innovation and productivity. And while email is an efficient communication tool, it is often misused—disguised as two-way communication when the true purpose is blaming, embarrassing someone or CYA. It's common to see all types of conflicts played out through emails, with an increasing audience of people who are copied. And often this takes place when the people involved are sitting just down the hall from each other.

It's common sense that two-way communication gathers more information, provides new perspectives, and avoids errors and confusion that can result in costly delays. While it takes more time on the front end, two-way communication saves time when plans and expectations are clear, when new ideas are introduced, and when questions can be asked. Two-way communication allows people to do it right the first time. It promotes trust and heightens employees' feelings of value that others have for them.

When leaders encourage two-way communication, it is imperative that they hold up their end of the process by listening. People quickly recognize when they are being asked for their opinion simply to satisfy a leader's feeling of obligation. Listening must be sincere, and it must be *active*. When actively listening, leaders ask more questions, probe for more information, and strive for clear understanding. And when clarification is needed, paraphrasing ensures that the intended message has been accurately received.

This approach is often used by parents. When Ken was a young father, he wanted to be the best dad he could be. He attended a course on parent effectiveness, and the trainers were stressing the importance of active listening and paraphrasing. He was home one afternoon when his six-year-old daughter Laura walked into the house, slammed the door, and said, "I hate Mrs. Johnson."

The traditional Ken would have responded with, "Don't slam that door, young lady, and don't talk that way about Mrs. Johnson!" But now that he was intent on being the best dad he could be, he instead said, "You seem upset. Did something bad happen at school today?"

"Yes," she sobbed. "And everyone was laughing at me."

Still practicing, he asked, "So you said something funny?"

"No," she wailed. "I was waving my hand and waving my hand, and she wouldn't call on me."

Realizing what had happened, he quietly asked, "Did you have an accident?" Laura nodded with tears streaming down her face. As he hugged her tightly, he realized that sincerely and actively listening at times of conflict or high emotion was not only effective at home but would also make him more effective at work.

Adults Want to be Treated Like Adults

Think about two neighbors. Let's call them Hank and Joe. They like each other. Maybe they're not best friends, or they don't socialize together much, but they get along with each other—small talk when they're out doing yard work, wave as they come and go, and occasionally lend each other a tool.

What would Hank do if Joe did something that irritated or annoyed him? Maybe Joe regularly parks on the street with his car extending a few feet past the edge of Hank's driveway. Or Joe leaves his plastic recycle bins sitting by the curb for days after they have been emptied. Now, remember, Hank and Joe really like each other and have had a great relationship. Would Hank be visibly upset toward Joe? Would he raise his voice or talk to him in a demeaning way? Probably not. Or, more accurately, *definitely* not.

Hank would either decide it isn't a big enough problem and let it go, or he would talk to Joe. He'd tell him what is bothering him and ask him if he could park his car differently or move the recycle bins. Because what would happen if he didn't react that way? What if he was accusatory or demeaning or even threatening? Most likely, their relationship would be damaged. Maybe irreparably. Interactions would become strained and less frequent. Those backyard chats would be a thing of the past. The friendly waves in the morning and evening would become shorter or nonexistent. And, as often happens with neighbors who choose this path, the relationship may never be the same.

If people make an effort in their personal lives to maintain good relationships and to find ways to calmly and rationally solve issues and conflicts, why doesn't that happen more often in the workplace? What changes when people get to work?

Ken says the best way to summarize the essence of adult-to-adult communication is:

Talk to people like you would to a neighbor you like.

Good neighbors don't always agree. They often don't even socialize. But they treat each other with respect and confront their differences accordingly.

Let's look at an example of two emails that were sent by leaders in two different companies:

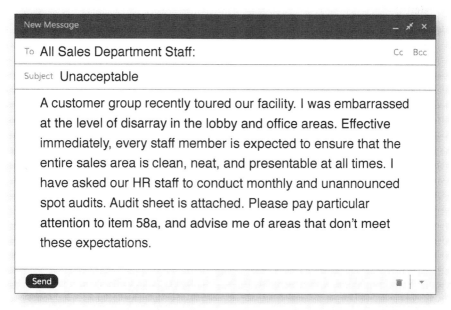

New Message   — ⚹ ✕

To   All Sales Department Staff: Cc   Bcc

Subject   Unacceptable

A customer group recently toured our facility. I was embarrassed at the level of disarray in the lobby and office areas. Effective immediately, every staff member is expected to ensure that the entire sales area is clean, neat, and presentable at all times. I have asked our HR staff to conduct monthly and unannounced spot audits. Audit sheet is attached. Please pay particular attention to item 58a, and advise me of areas that don't meet these expectations.

Send

Compare that with:

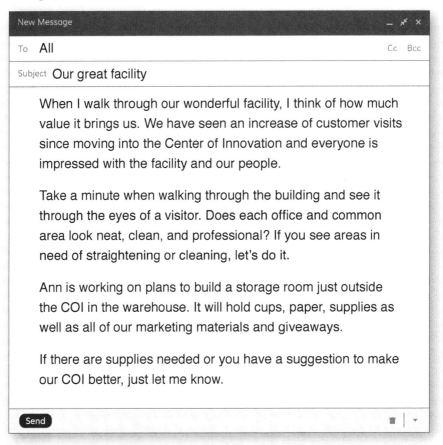

What is the difference? Is one memo demeaning while the other asks for involvement and ideas and commitment? Which memo is addressing the readers in an adult-to-adult tone—the way in which you would *talk to a neighbor you like?*

Leaders, educators, and trainers have long proclaimed the importance of good communication in the workplace. And communication forums and practices are in a constant state of transformation. While positive assumptions are *foundational* to creating a high-performance environment, open, two-way, adult-to-adult communication is *fundamental* to building the kind of relationships that are essential to achieving it.

Reply to All, Part Two

Robert, the director of operations, read the two emails with some exasperation. Two adults were behaving disrespectfully in full view of the entire executive staff. Since WPG had started transitioning its forty-year traditional culture to one that operated from the eight elements of HPWP, there were many examples in which the old management habits were still hard to break.

Robert's first thought was to examine his assumptions about Sal and Mike. Robert knew that Sal had been with the company for over twenty-five years and was still autocratic in his approach, even with the company's investment in leadership training for him. Mike was relatively new and had a lot of potential—a clear replacement for Sal as Sal moved toward retirement. Both were attentive to detail and met expectations, although Mike's communication and involvement of others routinely produced better results.

Robert walked into Sal's office. He could see the anxiety on Sal's face and immediately tried to put him at ease by smiling and relaxing in one of the chairs. "I just read your memo to Mike. Is that a discussion you two could have had in person?"

"Well, I guess," sighed Sal. "I'm just so frustrated with Mike's lack of communication."

Robert was direct. "As leaders here, our expectations are to not use email in a way that is disrespectful or causes conflict or embarrassment. You copied all the executives as well, which is not constructive. I saw Mike's email as well. What's your plan for moving forward?"

"I need to go talk to Mike in person. I'll do it now."

Mike was still angry when Sal walked into his office. "I wish you would have come to me before publishing that email for the world to see. You didn't even have all the facts," Mike said.

Sal sat down. "You're right. Let me start by saying that I used poor judgment in copying the others. In fact, I should have just come to you first regarding the cause of the delay. This all could have been avoided. But I have been frustrated that you aren't keeping me up to speed on the project."

Mike slammed his hands on the desk. "Then why didn't you tell me that?"

Sal paused and kept his temper in check. "I can see you're frustrated as well. Let's start over. We're both adults, and we both have a common goal—the success of this project. To start, I will come directly to you if I have questions or concerns and I ask that you do the same. Is it a deal?"

Mike paused, then grinned. "Sure," he said. "I guess the pressure is getting to me." Sal went back to his office, and as he sat down his phone rang. It was Mike. "Hey, Sal," he said, "Do you have time to help me with this one change request? It doesn't look like it will work."

"Sure," Sal replied. "I'll be right there."

CHAPTER **8**

Engage and Involve Employees

The Warehouse Renovations

Valissa scanned the floor plans for the warehouse renovations that were spread out on her desk. Since she had started her job as a forklift operator twelve years earlier, she had always sought ways to make the warehouse operations more efficient. Now that she had moved up to warehouse manager, she continued to focus even more on process improvements.

Last year, after three months of careful planning, she came up with a plan for rearranging all the material racks. She followed that with relocating temporary inventory storage. She felt that both changes were good, even though she heard some of the usual grumbling from employees who didn't seem to share that view. While she felt the workflow had improved, the efficiencies she had anticipated didn't seem to be confirmed in performance numbers.

Now she had made plans to move her office, and those of the other supervisors, to the mezzanine level. This would clear out additional space on the warehouse floor for equipment storage, an expanded break room, and another series of racks for an expanding product line. She was certain this arrangement would be well received by the employees. She sent a memo to all employees about the upcoming project, and she was looking forward to seeing their excitement Monday morning when the first construction crew showed up to begin the work.

Several weeks passed as the work continued, and she hadn't really seen the enthusiasm she was expecting from the shift workers. One afternoon, she approached one of the line employees who had only been with the company a few months. "Hi, Jarod. How's everything going?"

"Great, Val," he said, without looking away from his work.

"Well, are you excited about all the new changes?" she asked

"Sure, I guess. I haven't seen the plans, but I'm sure it will be good. Whatever you think works best for us." He looked up at Valissa and grinned. "Not that it's my concern, but down the road, you might consider rearranging the material racks and moving the temporary inventory storage location. I don't know whose idea it was to put them where they are, but

> most of us think it's really inefficient and causes a lot of double-handling."
>
> Valissa thanked him and went back to her office. She sat down, looked through a cloud of construction dust, and sighed. "People always find something to complain about."

The Cost of Low Engagement

Your company wouldn't purchase a piece of equipment or new technology with the intention of only using a fraction of its capability, right? So, let's go back to the scorecard you may have completed in chapter 1. What percent of an employee's potential is used in the job? What percent of an employee's brainpower is used on the job? When workshop participants are asked these questions, the numbers are rarely above 50 percent. Almost certainly, no leader would be satisfied with that percent of capability or capacity if they were looking at a process, system, or machine in their organization.

If it's the job of leaders to maximize performance, doesn't that mean maximizing human capital? Leaders must be focused on managing the cost of human capital to get the maximum return on that investment.

Barriers to Employee Engagement

A positive assumption about leaders today is that they are not frightened or intimidated by their team members having new or innovative ideas. There are, however, three significant barriers responsible for the 70 percent of our workforce that is disengaged.

1. **Engagement is Not a Job Expectation**

   Many companies promote from within, and candidates receiving these internal promotions are often selected according to their loyalty, responsibility, and knowledge or technical expertise (as well as time spent in their current job). This is particularly true of front-line leaders who have the largest day-to-day interaction with most of the workforce.

   We'll talk more about high-performance job expectations in chapter 11, but a critical issue with our front-line leaders is that they're not *expected* to facilitate engagement or promote employee empowerment. Can we agree that the people doing the job eight to ten hours a day most often know the job best? If so, how are our front-line leaders tapping into that knowledge for purposes of process improvements, cost-reduction ideas, and innovative solutions to problems? That aspect of the job, that ability, is not defined during the selection process. This results in placing good people who often lack the interest, ability, or skill set to practice employee engagement in key positions. And if engagement is a stretch, it is almost impossible for this group to visualize empowerment.

2. **It's Not What Your Boss Asks About**

   Frequently, higher levels of management are more focused on the day-to-day operation of the business than they should be. When a higher-level manager meets with his or her team to talk about production, quality, service, shipments, etc., the content of those meetings is concentrated on data and facts: What are our sales today? Are shipments on time? What are our efficiencies? If that's what your manager asks about, then consequently, that's where you will focus your time and attention.

When was the last time your manager asked, "What did you do today to engage your employees in ideas for cost reductions? What innovative ideas have your employees or team members raised? How is your team working together to solve problems?" If managers and leaders ask questions about *what* is getting done, the *how* will not be the focus. Employee involvement is the *how*, and it's the very best way to get things done.

3. **Leaders Don't Know How to Engage**

Experienced facilitators have invested hours and hours of education and practice in learning how to challenge thinking and promote collaboration. Very few newly-promoted, or even seasoned leaders, have had this type of training. Shepherding a group of individuals from point A to point B requires a complete set of facilitation skills, a rich toolbox of techniques and group processes, and experience that is honed by working with diverse groups on varying subjects. As our business environments evolve, this is fast becoming a critical competency for leaders.

Looking for Opportunities

Because traditional leaders often approach employee involvement from a more autocratic perspective, numerous opportunities to engage employees are dismissed or overlooked. When leaders have the mindset to expand engagement, these opportunities become apparent and abundant. Here's a simple guideline: if a company or management decision affects an employee, then that employee should, on some level, be involved in that decision.

Here are a few of the workplace processes and procedures in which talented, empowered employees are fully capable of engaging:

- Identifying problems that exist with productivity, quality, and safety process, and finding solutions

- Providing significant input and ideas for marketing and company growth

- Setting their own performance goals and objectives

- Selecting new employees using hiring teams

- Selecting their team supervisors and managers

- Developing team and company best work practices

- Coaching, counseling, and providing performance feedback to their peers

During our leadership workshops, participants are asked to debate the pros and cons of employees having the final decision in hiring their leader. Usually, the cons win the debate, using arguments such as, "they'll pick their friends," or, "they'll want someone who will be easier on them," or, "they don't have the skill sets to make that decision." These arguments, of course, are based on negative assumptions, and leaders must challenge traditional thinking and be mindful of the potential and brainpower of their employees that is going untapped; consider, for example, how sports team leaders are chosen and how our government officials are elected—although this may not be the best example of success. People in nonleadership positions are often given opportunities to participate in decisions that affect them.

A similar exercise has teams debating the pros and cons of employees making the final decision during a company layoff. Again, negative assumptions about people's motivations and behaviors are the heart of the con debate. Consider that in criminal trial situations, a jury of peers makes penalty decisions that may include a decision regarding life or death. When shocking disasters like the sinking of the Titanic occur, people step up and make calm decisions about who will get in the boats and who will stay behind.

The purpose of these debates is to push leaders' thinking and encourage employee engagement in every decision that may affect them. While the groups may not always make the final decisions, leaders have engaged the groups' thoughts and ideas to arrive at the best decision possible. High-performing leaders look for opportunities to engage employees, not for obstacles.

The Payoff

In high-performance environments, as engagement grows, peers begin to address performance and attendance issues directly with each other instead of approaching a manager. When confronted with these issues in such environments, the manager simply asks, "Have you talked directly to her? You're both adults, and I'm confident you can work this out." This approach allows leaders to spend more time doing the things they are accountable for—improving and growing the business.

If leaders are looking for a quantitative return on investment from employee engagement, it is this—high-performing companies can do more with less. They can grow without adding proportional resources, and they can do this through attrition, not workforce reduction. Avoiding workforce reductions in a high-performance environment is fundamental to the HPWP philosophy. If becoming leaner and more efficient means that people lose their jobs, it's irrational to expect high levels of commitment to making these kinds of improvements. When someone leaves the company or is promoted, the high-performance leader gathers the team and asks what changes they would make in processes and workload if they were not able to replace the departing team member. The predominant response of the team is to identify inefficiencies, remove redundancies, and streamline processes that can produce the same results or better without a replacement. And the team takes pride in and is motivated by its ability to do this.

> *If leaders are looking for a quantitative return on investment from employee engagement, it is this— high-performing companies can do more with less.*

Engagement means a change in mindset and vocabulary. Leaders shouldn't *let* people be engaged; they should proactively encourage and promote engagement. And while all the high-performance elements combine to create an environment where people want to come to work, the most critical element that creates loyalty and motivation is *engagement*. When organizations and leaders begin to *involve* people, they experience loyalty, motivation, and *commitment*. Everyone wins.

The Warehouse Renovations, Part Two

Valissa had arrived early Monday morning. As she sat at the break room table having a quiet cup of coffee, she thought about the leadership workshop she had attended the week before.

"Employees should be involved in every decision that affects them," she said quietly, repeating the words of the workshop facilitator. She had been thinking about that all weekend and had started formulating a plan to change her approach. She had always been the one to set the goals for her teams, and she continually tried to solve all the warehouse problems. She thought about what she could gain by getting them more involved in solving problems or making decisions. Even in hiring their coworkers.

When Valissa got to her office, she opened her binder and reviewed the notes she had made over the weekend. There were two issues she was going to focus on immediately—material storage and office locations. She had already laid out her plan for addressing the material storage issue. Thinking about what Jarod had told her—the inefficiencies and double-handling created by her original solution—she was going to meet with him and four other line employees that afternoon. She still had some concern that, when she solicited their input, the employees would come up with ideas and solutions that weren't feasible. Or maybe just crazy. Then she would have to tell them, "no," or at least redirect them. She reminded herself about having positive assumptions, and the importance of engagement, and knew that this was the right thing to do.

The meeting started promptly at 2:00 p.m. and Valissa began by letting the employees know how much she valued their input and ideas. Then she smiled and said, "Jarod has already pointed out to me that my ideas for the material racks and temporary storage locations weren't the best."

Jarod looked up, somewhat stunned. "That was your idea? I didn't know. I'm really sorry. I mean, I guess I can see why you decided to do that."

Valissa interrupted. "Don't worry Jarod. I'm glad you told me. And that's exactly why I wanted you all here to talk about this. You are the ones who know more about what works and what doesn't. So, let's talk about that."

After an hour, Valissa had flipcharts and pads full of notes and diagrams. As everyone got up to leave, she thanked them again for their openness and input. "Let me organize this information, and we can meet again Friday to review it. Does that work for everyone?" They all agreed to the follow-up meeting.

Jarod was the last to leave the room. As he walked by Valissa, he stopped. "Everyone really appreciates this.

And I think the ideas we came up with can really make a difference." He paused. "And I am really sorry about not liking your ideas," he smiled.

"I'm glad you didn't," she replied. "If you had, today's meeting might not have happened."

Over the next three months, Valissa continued to hold weekly meetings with various members of the production group. They would not only work on solving issues that Valissa presented to them, but had begun to create their own list of topics to discuss. During that time, her confidence in their ability to handle issues and problems that came up in the warehouse continued to grow.

Late one afternoon, as Valissa was preparing to leave, Jarod stepped in to her office. "Say, Val," he said. "Me and a few of the packers would like to stay a couple of hours and try out the new stacking system that we talked about. Is that all right with you?"

"Sure," Valissa said. "Don't stay too long."

"We won't," Jarod said. "We'll let you know in the morning how it worked. Have a great evening."

As she walked to her car, she thought, "I *will* have a great evening. There is certainly nothing to worry about here."

CHAPTER **9**
Conduct Exceptional Training

Welcome to Your Overwhelming New Job

As Todd drove through the gate of Caldwell Transportation's service center, he remembered that he had a new driver manager trainee coming in at 7:00. He hopped out of his truck, grabbed some coffee as he went through the break room, and started toward his office. He glanced over near the front entrance and noticed a man sitting on one of the metal chairs by the door.

Todd paused. "Can I help you?"

"Yeah. I'm Drew. I was told to be here at 7:00 for training."

"OK, well, you're just a little earl..." Todd looked at the wall clock above the door as he spoke. "Oh, I guess it's ten after already. Well, hold tight there and we'll get started."

Drew was a recent college graduate with a degree in operations and was anxious to put his education to work. Caldwell had an excellent reputation for valuing people and investing in professional growth. Over the next two days, Drew's excitement grew as he learned about Caldwell's history, services, and culture. He engaged in interactive games and quizzes, took tours of the facility, and was introduced to employees and leaders who were very accommodating in answering his questions, helping him learn, and making him feel welcome.

The final phase of Drew's training involved shadowing other driver managers, learning the specific system that supported dispatching loads, and assisting drivers in being personally and financially successful.

Drew's enthusiasm quickly turned to panic. As he sat down next to Nate, his peer trainer, he saw a dozen computer screens with constantly changing information. As Nate's fingers flew over the keyboard, he explained the dispatching process to Drew, all while taking phone calls and regularly accessing new information on the screens. Drew attempted to take notes, but everything was happening too fast. He felt embarrassed to ask questions and didn't want to interrupt Nate. His anxiety grew as he became more overwhelmed with the requirements and details of the process. He began to think that the driver manager position might not be a good match for him.

While having a highly skilled and committed workforce is key to optimizing success, training is often de-emphasized in companies in terms of importance and investment. And the lack of solid on-the-job training is often cited as a reason for turnover. So why is training often seemingly undervalued by senior leadership?

Good Training and Bad Training

Despite numerous subject matter experts (SMEs) in a company, few have been taught basic training design principles and adult learning theory. When these experts are asked to develop a training course, they often put everything they know on wordy PowerPoint slides, in fonts too small to read, with sound effects that quickly become annoying. Participants who attend training like this usually refer to it as "Death by PowerPoint."

Effective training is often viewed as costly, both in terms of the time required to design good training techniques and materials as well as the time trainees spend going through the process. While time and materials cost money, companies *must* view it as an investment. Companies with large training departments are usually able to measure the impact of training both qualitatively and quantitatively.

But not all companies make this investment or have access to this resource. Good training starts with identifying a clear, measurable gap between actual performance and desired performance. But it is also important to identify the cause of the performance gap. Often the discrepancy in performance can be due to causes other than a lack of training, such as unclear expectations, lack of feedback, flawed systems, or competing priorities. In these cases, spending time and money in training is a non-value-added cost and doesn't solve the performance issue. When it becomes clear that training is the most appropriate solution, training experts then define the performance objectives; i.e., what will the learner be able to *do* after completing training. Only then is a training solution, using adult learning principles and sometimes multimedia, if appropriate, created.

Training generally falls into three buckets: Leadership training, technical or on-the-job training, and team skills training.

Leadership Training

There are many wonderful leadership training programs that have been designed in-house or are available for purchase from external vendors. Most of the training is skill-based and addresses needed leadership competencies. This type of training has value, but leadership development through effective training needs to go deeper.

Human Resources organizations are frequently called on to provide management training. Jenna was an employee relations representative for a large aerospace company. She was responsible for ensuring that 120 supervisors and managers followed myriad company policies. Most of the management staff she worked with were good people who hadn't read the specific policies and procedures associated with managing their teams. New to her job, she was asked to provide training in this area. She couldn't think of anything more boring than walking them through the manual, so instead, she created various scenarios that called on the trainees to discuss how best to handle these different employee situations. Not only were the participants highly engaged, but they started questioning why the policies were so strict and often prevented them from following what common sense and good judgment would have told them to do. It seemed to Jenna that providing this kind of training, with follow-on interactive discussions where front-line and middle management could openly discuss actual situations, would provide a higher level of learning regarding how to manage the workforce. And it was determined that most of the restrictive policies could be eliminated. Many of the policies had been created based on the assumption that supervisors, and even managers, couldn't be trusted to use common sense and good judgment. And rather than invest in training and coaching to develop the competencies required by these policies, it had been easier to provide a step-by-step procedure on how to handle employee concerns, problems, questions, and requests.

That's the kind of leadership training needed for today's leaders. Assuming the competency of front-line leaders (who impact most of an organization's staff and employees) is the preexisting foundation for employee retention and achievement, then quality experiential training is critical.

In a high-performance workplace, management training is not limited to practicing a set of skills and learning the organization's policies. It's structured to drive this important group of leaders to listen, question and *think* through each issue; to use their resources and each other to explore alternatives; and to arrive at a decision that is fair to the employee and in the best interests of the company.

Skill training moves the performance needle, but only a little. It's when people in leadership positions understand the importance of their roles and are free to use critical thinking skills and good judgment that their performance and the performance of their teams achieve significantly higher results.

Technical Training

A HPWP midwestern milling operation had just been notified of two serious quality errors that, fortunately, were recoverable. This set off a major internal alarm because the cause could be traced to employee error due to lack of sound training. As the company had grown, training was passed from a more experienced person to the new hire through informal verbal instruction and demonstration. Once the new hire was competent, he or she was now apt to become the trainer for another new hire. As with the telephone game, the message tended to become distorted. Important processes were unintentionally overlooked, and trainers often assumed that the new hire would "just know" the basics.

Often, technical training consists of a peer trainer first telling a new hire what is going to be done, then demonstrating—or describing what he or she is doing while doing it. This is often followed by, "Do you have any questions?" New to the job, most people simply nod, not wanting to appear as if they haven't paid attention or aren't very smart. The trainer, who has other full-time responsibilities, then leaves, encouraging the trainee to find the peer trainer if there are any questions or problems.

In contrast, the *Tell-Tell, Show-Show* approach, works like this:

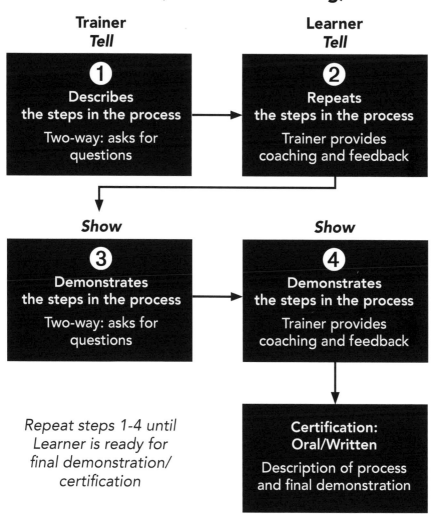

Tell-Tell, Show-Show Model for OJT (On-The-Job Training)

Trainer
Tell

①
**Describes
the steps in the process**

Two-way: asks for
questions

Learner
Tell

②
**Repeats
the steps in the process**

Trainer provides
coaching and feedback

Show

③
**Demonstrates
the steps in the process**

Two-way: asks for
questions

Show

④
**Demonstrates
the steps in the process**

Trainer provides
coaching and feedback

*Repeat steps 1-4 until
Learner is ready for
final demonstration/
certification*

**Certification:
Oral/Written**

Description of process
and final demonstration

After the trainer has put the learner at ease, described the importance of the task, the effect of errors, and the tell-tell-show-show nature of the training, the following steps are used.

- **Step One:** The trainer *describes* the steps in a specific task using a listing of these tasks, so the learner sees and hears the steps. In general, this is done in a quiet place, away from the work site.

- **Step Two**: The trainer then asks the learner to *repeat* the steps in the task—coaching when an item is missed or incorrect—until both feel very confident that the learner clearly *understands* the process.

- **Step Three**: The trainer takes the learner to the worksite and *demonstrates* the steps in the task.

- **Step Four:** The learner then *shows* the trainer how to perform the steps in the task.

- When both trainer and learner feel confident in the learning, the trainer certifies the learner in that task and either goes on to teach new tasks or the learner continues to perform this task.

The milling company mentioned earlier immediately started analyzing its on-the-job training process and realized that many Standard Operating Procedures (SOPs) weren't used in training or were out of date. Using interns and involving their employee experts, SOPs were converted to on-line training manuals, complete with detailed steps and photographs. A small cadre of current employees, staff, and management were trained as technical trainers in this model.

The company continued to use this approach and, while having more steps than traditional training, this method cut training time by one-third to one-half. The need to repeat what the trainer was saying required learners to listen more carefully and ask more questions, thus gaining a thorough understanding of what was expected. This built confidence for both the trainer and the learner. Watching the learner demonstrate the competencies required to perform the task several times drove even higher levels of confidence and competence.

Companies should invest the time to create SOPs for all jobs, then transform them into training documents that are routinely monitored for updates. Then choose peer trainers carefully. In addition to technical knowledge, these trainers need strong interpersonal communication skills, good judgment in ascertaining the learner's level of comprehension, and patience.

Team Skills

In high-performance workplaces, employees are highly engaged in solving problems, increasing productivity, and working as a team. The operations manager of one high-performing company was talking with the human resources director when a group of production employees walked down the hall, heading for a conference room. The HR director called out to one of the team members and asked if there was something going on. "Oh, we're just having a short meeting with one of our team members who seems to be having trouble getting to work on time. We can take care of it," she said and smiled.

In a work environment where team leaders focus on planning, process improvement, eliminating barriers, and team member development, the day-to-day performance of the team is left to the team members. These are teams with a common vision and high expectations of each other. They are expected to be resourceful, thoughtful, and collaborative. And they are expected to manage themselves according to the company's values. As important as technical skills are, communication skills are equally critical. The ability to coach and provide feedback to peers usually requires training and practice and is a hallmark of any high-performing team.

Welcome to Your Overwhelming New Job, Part Two

Todd was at his desk early that morning preparing for the arrival of a new driver manager trainee. In the seven months since he had attended the High Performance Leadership Workshop, he had completely changed Caldwell's approach to onboarding, and specifically to on-the-job training. Along with implementing the *Tell-Tell-Show-Show* model with all peer trainers, an action team had also created standard operating procedures for all the driver-related processes. Todd knew it would take some time to see positive results, and he had to be patient.

As Todd was going over the new hire's information that morning, his phone rang. It was Nate, one of the peer trainers. Nate told Todd that they had scheduled two more new driver trainees to come in that morning and he needed to get them up to speed as quickly as possible. There were new plans coming in faster than the current driver managers could handle. Todd suggested that, just for this time, they deviate from the model and just have the trainees shadow the trainer for the day, as they had done in the past.

Todd agreed and hung up the phone. He sat at his desk for a minute, then picked up the phone again and called Nate.

"Let's not do that, Nate. We've been working on this, and the results we're getting are great. If we start cutting corners now, I'm concerned that we'll keep doing that. We're always going to need our new drivers up and running quickly, but I don't want to shortcut this."

"We can still go back when we have time and do *Tell-Tell-Show-Show*," Nate pushed back.

"It won't be the same. And I doubt that we would ever find time to go back and do it. Let's stick with our model. We know it works."

"Sounds good," Nate said. "But can you call the planners and let them know? They were expecting us to have driver managers available to dispatch sooner rather than later."

"I'll take care of it," Todd said. He smiled and hung up the phone.

It was nearing the end of the first full year of implementing the *Tell-Tell-Show-Show* training method. Todd sat at his desk looking at the quarterly report and the year-to-date numbers, especially the critical metrics that Caldwell tracked. The results had exceeded his expectations. Among the new driver managers that year, there had been a 32-percent reduction in safety incidents, a 74-percent reduction in the turnover rate, and an 18-percent increase in on-time deliveries.

As he continued to review the report, he was simultaneously running numbers in his head—the cost savings that these metrics represented was astounding. He picked up the phone to call Nate. Nate had become a champion of the new training model, and Todd wanted to congratulate him and let him know the impact Nate and the other peer trainers were having.

Nate was excited about the information and the difference they had been able to make through the new process. He thanked Todd for his support, and before they hung up, he had one more thing to tell him.

"Todd, I also wanted to let you know that the last two driver managers we hired said they applied here because of what they had been told about our great training program. One of them told me that, at his last job, they basically sat him in front of a computer and told him to figure it out. He said he really appreciated the time we were investing in them. Thanks for keeping us focused on this."

Todd grinned as he sat the phone down. "Wow," he said. "That used to be me."

CHAPTER **10**

Ensure Competitive Wages and Benefits

What Is Everybody Worth?

Joe is enjoying the single life. He lives in a socially active part of town and spends a fair amount of his pay on entertainment. In fact, his life is near-perfect now that he's been working at DeskTop, which is just a short bike ride from his downtown condo. He started working there after graduating college as an associate buyer and after only six months was promoted to senior buyer. He remembers arriving for his interview and walking into this giant, open space with exposed pipes and ductwork running across high ceilings. There was a coffee bar to the right. He could see immediately that teams worked together—many were standing, while other small groups talked enthusiastically in different lounge settings with sofas and easy chairs. He could feel the energy. After joining the company, his first impressions were further reinforced by the clear signs of business growth and ongoing collaboration among different groups. He couldn't imagine a better place to work.

Then one day, just one little piece of information changed his perspective.

The company didn't have a published salary structure, but that hadn't been a problem for Joe because he felt he was being paid competitively. But that day, Lisa, the company's staffing manager, had accidentally left an offer letter for a new senior buyer in the copy machine. Joe had been waiting to use the copier and found the letter. What he saw had made him do a double-take. The company planned to bring someone in at his level at a significantly higher rate of pay. All the good things about working at DeskTop faded as he immediately felt devalued.

Meanwhile, Lisa, having discovered her mistake, raced back to the copier to find the letter sitting on top for anyone to see. The salary offer was high, but the candidate had years of experience and would be able to hit the ground running. Because salary information was private, she hoped no one had seen the letter.

Most people who are educated, skilled, and experienced can find another job that pays more money. It may take some longer than others, but if they are driven toward that goal, they will most likely achieve it. So why isn't everyone continuously searching for the next, better-paying job?

Here's an example that provides an explanation. Bonnie, a veteran outside-management consultant, was trying to gauge the level of employee satisfaction with a company that had heavily invested in creating a culture of trust and high performance. Facing a large group of hourly-paid employees, she started by asking, "How many people would leave their current job for $500 per month?" No hands raised.

"What about $ 750 per month?" Two people out of forty-five raised their hands.

Somewhat surprised, she asked, "What about $1,000 per month?" Four more people raised their hands.

"OK. What about $2,000 per month?" Another few hands went up.

"Don't you all want to make more money?" she asked.

Carl, a man in the front row, looked around the room and then stood up. "This company values us as people. We're involved in changes. We're expected to solve problems and make decisions. We know how the company is performing and we celebrate progress and success. I feel like an owner. If I'm paid fairly for what I do, it's hard to imagine going back to a job where I'm nothing but a number to the management and no one gives a crap about my ideas and opinions. I know people who are supervisors and some managers that don't have as much autonomy as I do." Many in the room nodded in agreement.

Make Pay a Nonissue

Conduct any online search for factors affecting employee retention, and pay is not in the top three. If people feel they are being paid fairly, it will be other factors—dislike for their boss, lack of challenging work and professional development, and work/home life imbalance—that will cause them to seek other opportunities. The goal in a high-performance workplace is to make pay a *nonissue*, and leaders must use these four components to achieve that:

- Pay competitively based on market data

- Separate the value of the job from the value of the person

- Maintain a simple compensation structure

- Be transparent regarding the structure and market data survey results

Pay Competitively

It does not make sense to be the highest-paying employer because this can dramatically affect profitability—particularly in down times. Conversely, it's also poor business to be a low-paying employer and unable to attract and retain good people. As Ken says, companies do not make money off what they don't pay their employees.

A very subtle thing happens when companies try to pay less. They *expect* less. And they get less. Ed was an easygoing, middle-aged CFO of a medical device company. The customer service department reported

> Companies do not make money off what they **don't** pay their employees.

to him. There had been many complaints about the customer service manager from those who reported to her as well as from a few customers. When asked why he wasn't addressing these issues, he responded, "She may not be great, but then again, I'm not paying her much."

People view competitive pay as fair pay. If they search, they can find another employer who will pay more. But if they like the environment in which they work, they won't leave unless the opportunity presented is one too difficult to refuse.

Jobs Have Market Value; People Are Priceless

First, leaders need to be clear that every job has a market value. Particularly in startup or small, private companies, the employees who help build the business are highly valued by the owners. They are willing to do most anything to help the business succeed, and it is hard to place a title or job description on this contribution. Often, owners show their appreciation through pay.

Juan, a hard-working warehouse manager in a California bouquet operation, had been instrumental in helping the owner grow the business over the past five years. As the company became more and more profitable, Phil, the owner, gave Juan large pay increases. This was fine until Phil's company merged with another, much larger, company. The managing partner of the new business venture reviewed Phil's operation and learned that Juan's salary was $30,000 over the top of the company's range for a warehouse manager. (Phil had never had a compensation structure.) To Phil, Juan was invaluable. To the managing partner, Juan was a well-performing warehouse manager who was substantially overpaid and would create internal equity issues with the other warehouse managers. Ultimately, Juan's salary was significantly decreased, and Phil was sure he'd lose him. However, Juan's limited experience as a warehouse manager of a small company prevented him from finding a similar job that paid even *close* to what he was currently making. In the end, a dispirited Juan remained with the company. Having lost his passion and commitment, his performance deteriorated so much that Phil eventually had to terminate his employment.

In this case, Juan would have been better prepared had Phil shown his appreciation by developing him—giving him more responsibility and publicly and privately communicating his gratitude for Juan's loyalty and flexibility. Phil had unintentionally put Juan in a position from which he never recovered.

A Compensation Structure

Juan's story is a relatively common scenario for companies that don't have a compensation structure. Without the structure, conversations about pay get muddy as the discussion becomes about the person's value and contribution. The pay decision becomes subjective, and managers often either provide the requested increase or fumble through some ambiguous rationale regarding why there won't be an increase. This is easily fixed with a clean compensation structure created by establishing pay ranges for company jobs that match similar jobs in terms of the regional market demand for this occupation. Salary surveys are conducted every year or every other year to see how the value of a job may have changed. For example, as technology has advanced, the need for jobs requiring IT knowledge and experience has increased dramatically. When the talent available is not plentiful enough to meet demand, the value of the job increases to attract and retain this talent.

Today, survey data is available through any number of sources. The relatively small cost of obtaining this data is easily recovered when a manager can use information versus opinion to help determine an individual's pay compared to job responsibilities.

OK, so now there is a clear compensation structure. What about the people who are earning a salary that is above the maximum in the current range? There are many factors managers should consider:

1. **What is the potential for further professional development?** If there is high potential, find challenging assignments or stretch roles. When a higher-level (and higher-paying) job becomes available, the individual will be ready for it.

2. **Look at the work.** Are there opportunities to combine jobs and cross-train, resulting in a higher-level contributor position? Look for opportunities to broaden job responsibilities in a tangible and meaningful way (not a surface way to simply justify more money).

3. **What if a person has been in the job for years, is good at it, doesn't want to change jobs, but wants to continue to get good increases every year?** This is tougher. Compensation analysts suggest that once a person's pay falls outside the range for the job, the pay is red-circled, meaning there are no increases until the market value for the job has increased to the point that this person's pay now falls inside the range. Another approach is to give high performers annual lump-sum amounts instead of a salary increase—thereby allowing companies to recognize good performance monetarily without increasing the base salary that is already out of range. In any circumstance,

it's incumbent on the manager to have a direct, adult-to-adult conversation about the company's system of compensation.

4. **Implement a profit-sharing program that includes everyone. All employees receive the same percentage.** (In some circumstances, higher-level managers already engaged in a bonus program may be exempted.) With profit-sharing, everyone is fairly compensated for their responsibilities, as well as being rewarded for their contributions.

At the same time, leaders must be cautious when implementing profit-sharing programs. Alex, the owner of a growing company in Southern California, wanted to implement profit-sharing for all the right reasons. The company had grown so fast, however, that the metrics weren't well developed. Having clear metrics that employees can impact, as well as regularly communicating performance to these metrics on a weekly or monthly basis, is critical. Alex moved forward with implementing profit-sharing. It was a less-than-profitable year, but Alex had never really communicated how the business was performing. In the end, Alex paid out profit-sharing even though there wasn't profit to share, and then terminated the program.

Be Transparent

Many companies choose not to share information related to compensation with their employees. (It's understood that personal pay information is and should be private. Compensation structure, pay grades, and competitive analysis survey results should be shared.) For some companies, information isn't shared because the structure doesn't exist yet, and there is hesitancy in developing a structure for fear that many people may be over- or undercompensated, and leaders are not sure how to handle that. Some companies have negative assumptions about how employees will handle this information. Whatever the reason, there's still a problem. People talk. They want to know if a job they are being offered is a promotion, demotion, or a lateral move. In the absence of information, they will make assumptions.

Share survey data. The first time it is made available, many people may want to see it. As time goes by and compensation becomes a nonissue, employees will come to trust the pay structure and only raise questions when they feel responsibilities have changed.

About Incentives

If a job in a company's industry is typically bonus-eligible (as it often is with management positions) or incentive-based (as it often is with sales positions), the company should maintain this structure to be competitive.

Some companies, however, use bonus and incentive systems for nonexempt positions (warehouse, office, operations, etc.) based on the belief that this will increase individual productivity. In a high-performance environment, this is *a negative assumption about the workforce*. Higher performance can be achieved by setting high expectations and involving people in how to reach them. In addition, individual performance incentives for nonexempt employees are not typically necessary to be competitive and have been proven to negatively impact quality and limit teamwork.

There are additional downsides to using incentives for productivity goals. Those who can demonstrate high productivity are able to earn more than others. So, what's wrong with that? For one thing, it causes direct supervisors to spend less time coaching less-productive employees.

The traditional thought is that if they want to make more, they'll need to work faster. If they don't, then they're only hurting themselves. How does a company foster an environment of high performance when leaders are willing to allow the incentive system to drive performance? It is the *leader* who should drive high performance by communicating high expectations.

Additionally, incentive systems create a what-have-you-done-for-me-lately mentality. When team members are asked to be part of a hiring team, they might ask what additional pay they'll receive for that. Or they might decline because it would hurt their incentive pay. In a high-performance environment, everyone is expected to support the company's objectives. Often this takes people out of their regular routine for a short time. These additional responsibilities should be viewed as opportunities, not as reasons for additional pay.

Finally, bonus and incentive programs can create conflicting goals between departments or company functions. Is a manager going to decide that something is in the best interest of the company when that decision will negatively impact her department's performance and her personal bonus? This creates territorialism, fostering a win/lose approach to working together.

Organizations should be very careful in establishing incentive systems because, once they're in, they are very difficult to remove or replace.

What is Everybody Worth, Part Two

Joe cooled down a little before he went to see Sarah, his boss, about the disparity in his pay and that of the new hire. While Sarah listened empathetically to his frustration, her immediate thought was her own frustration that Lisa would be so careless with private information. Sarah told Joe she would speak with Lisa. At that time, she didn't know any specific information that could help her address this.

Lisa was in her office working on the communication and training plan for a new compensation structure. Recruitment had been challenging due to fierce competition for talent. Having attended a conference that emphasized both the need for a great work culture along with competitive and transparent pay systems, she and her director were about to launch a process to give managers and supervisors an understanding of basic compensation theory and structure.

Sarah entered Lisa's office without knocking. "I've just had to deal with one of my best new performers who's upset because he saw an offer letter you left on the copier."

Lisa blushed and apologized profusely. "I was in a hurry, but that's no excuse. What did you tell him?"

"I didn't know what to tell him. I'm a manager in this company, and even I don't know how some of these decisions are made." Sarah said.

"I can understand your frustration. I'm working right now on a plan to educate and inform all our leaders how to make good compensation decisions and respond to employees who have questions. But let me help you deal with your situation first."

Lisa showed Sarah the survey data that had led to creating a compensation structure with pay ranges. She explained the midpoint in each range was the market value for the jobs in that range. Lisa asked Sarah if Joe was competently performing all aspects of a senior buyer role. While Sarah said he showed high potential, he was still in a learning mode at that level. The new candidate was near the top of the salary range, but Lisa pointed out that his experience justified the higher salary.

Sarah understood and wanted to show Joe the data. Lisa was reluctant to do that without approval from the human resources director.

Sarah went back to Joe and explained that the difference in pay was due to experience in that job. She reassured Joe that he was highly valued and that there continued to be great opportunities for him to grow in both his professional development and earning potential. He was somewhat mollified.

During the next six weeks, Joe worked with the new senior buyer and significantly developed his research and negotiating skills. In addition, Sarah met with her team and reviewed the compensation structure and how hiring and merit pay decisions were made. Joe was able to see that if he continued to perform at a high level, he would receive a higher percentage merit increase because his base pay was lower in the range. It all made sense to him now. It was the lack of understanding and transparency that had caused him to become disillusioned.

CHAPTER **11**
Establish High Expectations

The Letter of the Law versus the Spirit of the Law

Rhoda liked hands-on work and had never been really interested in going to college. While she enjoyed her work as a senior customer service representative for Hoskin Ramey Builders, her personal life was not what she had dreamed. This was the first company she had started working for straight out of high school. Still unmarried at thirty-five, she was becoming resentful that she had allowed her dedication to HRB to become more important than pursuing social opportunities. She was always the first to volunteer to work overtime, but was constantly frustrated that her hard work went unrecognized. When the opportunity for an internal promotion to the Human Resources department came up, she thought it was time for a change and actively campaigned to be considered for the position. She wasn't considered a superstar by her current manager, but he knew she had a great work ethic. Because she had been with the company for seventeen years and had been recognized for her skills at handing conflicts and working with people, she was given the opportunity.

The tasks listed in the job description for the human resources assistant included: Monitor attendance records and performance reviews, maintain and support regulatory and company policies, answer benefits questions, support employee recognition, and prepare the monthly company newsletter.

While she knew she'd have to learn more about regulatory issues, she felt confident in her ability to do the job. Her desk was in an open area where employees could come to her as their first point of contact when they had an employment-related question.

Three months after she had started the new position, Rhoda was not happy. She'd had a preliminary performance review with Sam, her boss and the human resources manager. He felt she still had a lot to learn in the areas of employee relations, and also in developing good relationships with the department supervisors she supported. From Rhoda's perspective, she was fulfilling all of her new responsibilities. She had learned the regulatory and company policies within the first week. She was on top of monitoring all the supervisors' attendance records and regularly admonished them to deal with absentee problems. Late performance reviews had decreased substantially due to her persistent follow-up. Her first three newsletters had been published on time. She had completed these tasks despite being constantly interrupted with employee questions throughout the day.

Sam was equally unhappy. He had hired Rhoda because of her ability to deal with conflict, but she seemed to be causing more conflict through her police-like approach in her work with supervisors. He agreed that she was aptly doing the tasks listed in the job description, yet he was concerned that she couldn't distinguish between results and tasks.

No one wants to settle for mediocrity. However, in our workshops, when we ask, "How many of you have employees who are just meeting the *minimum*?" almost everyone raises a hand (some raise *two*). And often, the minimum is accepted. When leaders don't set high expectations, they shouldn't be surprised when average results are achieved. If status quo is expected, then that unintentional goal—mediocrity—will be realized.

This is such an easy thing to change. Just *raise the minimum*. If leaders do nothing else than focus on what's in this chapter, they are guaranteed to increase performance.

Most people are relatively clear about their job responsibilities. What is frequently unclear is the expectation of *how well* they should perform these responsibilities. You will struggle to substantially and consistently improve individual and work team results if you don't do the following three things:

1. Set High Expectations

As with the other elements of HPWP, doing this requires leaders to have positive assumptions. If you believe people want to excel, want to win, and want to contribute, it is imperative to have higher expectations.

The job description or job profile is the most common method of communicating job responsibilities. The problem with traditional job descriptions is that they're usually just a list of tasks instead of a description of expected results. Tasks turn jobs into to-do lists. *Job profiles* that quantify the expected *results* turn task-oriented jobs into challenging careers.

Compare a portion of two job descriptions of one of our most common positions: the front-line supervisor in a production environment.

Supervisor	Team Leader
Supervise production line operation in accordance with plant policies and procedures. Train and coach production line employees.	Achieve record-breaking performance by continuously inspiring and developing a superior team that always produces the highest-quality products in the most cost-effective ways.

Now let's look at the impact these different descriptions have on the individual and the entire company. If a manager is hiring to the first description, he or she is likely to promote someone who is loyal, knowledgeable, and dependable from within the current workforce.

If that same manager applies the second description to the selection process, on the other hand, he or she will also be looking for someone with demonstrated leadership qualities—someone who inspires and motivates people. This may require looking outside the company. It's not necessarily that there aren't talented front-line workers; it's just that there may not have been a prior internal investment in their leadership development before there is a hiring need.

Review the words used in the second description: *record-breaking, continuously inspiring, superior team, always produces, highest quality, most cost-effective ways*. High-performance job profiles describe expected results using superlatives. This often elicits some resistance from management. Their pushback is generally phrased along the lines of, "if everything is described as ideal, and perfect, and the very best, then it's not real, and people won't be successful. They're just being set up to fail."

On the contrary: High expectations set people up to succeed. There is a difference between a performance goal or objective and an expectation for how it will be performed. Goals should be a stretch. They should challenge people to exceed what is considered standard performance. And they also must be attainable. The initiative and talent required to achieve these goals is a progression—one that demonstrates continued improvement. What should be the quality expectation for people assembling airplane parts? Doesn't it have to be 100 percent? Would a manufacturing leader choose to improve their safety record by 50 percent, going from ten lost-time accidents to five lost-time accidents? Or going from two deaths to one death? The expectation must be zero when it comes to safety. That doesn't mean it's a failure if safety records are improved but not perfect—but setting the highest expectation will drive maximum results.

High-Performance Work Places have extremely low absenteeism, and it can usually be attributed to the expectations that are set. Most such organizations pay everyone a salary, with no set number of sick days or paid time off (PTO). At first, it doesn't seem logical, or even possible, that an organization that pays all reasonable and necessary absences would have the lowest absenteeism rate. But they do.

When a company sets the expectation for attendance, and that everyone is to be at work every day, on time, the results are astounding. In a culture of high expectations, companies still recognize that something may happen that causes someone to miss work, but that doesn't change the expectation. If a problem with attendance does occur, an adult-to-adult, problem-solving discussion ensues.

So, what about PTO and sick days? Many companies establish a set number of sick days or PTO days, which is almost like extra vacation. These organizations are paying for absences that would not necessarily occur with established high-performance expectations. (Some companies even pay this time out if it's not used.)

In almost every traditional job description, one common statement is tacked on after listing all the standard tasks: "Other duties as assigned." Does that mean someone who finishes assigned tasks should wait to be told what to do next? And if nothing is "assigned," what does the person do? Not much. Statements like this unintentionally set minimum expectations. And that results in minimum performance.

Instead, high-performance job profiles end with, "Proactively support the organization's goals and objectives."

If this is the high expectation and someone isn't demonstrating intelligence, initiative, and teamwork, he or she is not meeting those expectations. This doesn't mean that person is not a good employee. It does mean that person's manager needs to find out what's getting in the way of performing at a high level, instead of simply settling for average performance.

Leaders and staffing people also get another, sometimes unanticipated, byproduct of these high-performance profiles—they are a great recruiting tool. High performers want to work in a stimulating environment. And using these challenging descriptions in online recruiting efforts will draw a higher caliber of candidates.

2. Communicate High Expectations

Setting high expectations is the first critical step. Communicating those expectations is essential to achieving them. And it isn't just telling people they need to work more, work harder, or work smarter. High expectations give people a purpose for their work, along with management's belief that they will be successful.

Leaders often believe they are setting high expectations, especially when it comes to assigning difficult or challenging assignments and projects. However, these assignments are often accompanied by one common, well-intended phrase:

"Do the best you can."

What could possibly be wrong with, "Do the best you can"? It certainly sends a message: just not one that communicates high expectations. The message here is, "This project will be very challenging. It would be difficult for anyone to complete it with the highest level of success. You represent our best hope."

This is a common phrase used by parents to encourage their children. Ken's daughter, Jenna, routinely came home from school and announced such things as a major science test at the end of the week. Proactively preparing her parents for a less-than-spectacular result, she confidently asserted the level of difficultly the test would present. Mom's supportive response was, "Do the best you can, honey." (Serious motivation, right?) Ken took a different approach. His response was, "Is it possible to get an A? If it's possible, is there any reason why you couldn't get an A? You know the material. You've done well in class so far. I'm looking forward to you getting an A." This challenge to her, and his belief in her capability, had a direct impact on her subsequently improved school performance. This same principle applies to the workplace.

Five years ago, a food manufacturing company hired Jordan as the manager to oversee the packaging area. He was chosen based on his previous work experience, his demonstrated leadership in the armed services, and a personality that people immediately liked and respected. At the time Jordon assumed responsibility for the department, they were performing at 45 percent efficiency, largely due to the age and poor condition of the equipment. Plans to improve the equipment and technology were over a year away, but management believed that efficiencies could still be improved through strong leadership. Jordan regularly challenged and supported his team and morale was good, but six months later, there was no change in efficiency. During this time, Jordan also engaged in several coaching sessions with his manager. Ultimately, it was mutually agreed that the job wasn't the right fit for Jordan, and he left the company on positive terms.

Upon Jordan's departure, Debra was internally promoted from the warehouse to Jordan's former position. Within two months of assuming the role, packaging efficiencies had increased from 45 percent to 70 percent. The head of operations was mystified and asked Debra what she had done differently to realize this magnitude of change. She said, "Jordan did a great job of setting high expectations and challenging the team, but I don't think he really *believed* it was possible with the current equipment. I knew this team could do it—even if they didn't think so at first." Debra's belief in the group, combined with her confident communication of high expectations, made the difference in the results that were achieved.

Communicating Belief

Consider a developing professional about to embark on a new project. When his manager tells him about it, she can take one of the following two approaches:

"I know this project is a stretch. There are a lot of unknowns, and we haven't done a lot of this type of work in the past. There are things you haven't learned yet, but I am here to try and help. Do the best you can."

Compare that to: "I specifically wanted to give this assignment to you. The things you will learn throughout this project will accelerate your development. I am excited by the talent and creative thinking that you have demonstrated and can bring to this project. Please use me as a resource whenever you need to. I'm really looking forward to the results."

Which would this developing professional find more motivating?

As leaders, you can also use high-performance job profiles as motivation for reaching higher levels of achievement. But you can't let the profile be a piece of paper that gets filed away and never looked at. Regularly use these job profiles to assess progress, and reinforce high expectations and confidence, as part of every employee's personal development.

3. Follow-Up: Coach for Higher Performance

If there is limited (or no) feedback that follows the first two steps (setting and communicating high expectations), individual progress won't be maximized. It might be a little better, but it won't have the same result as it would with a leader skilled at providing constructive feedback and positive reinforcement.

Positive Reinforcement

"Good job." We have all heard this. Typically, it's at the end of the day as our boss heads home. People want to be recognized for their contributions, and "good job" is a start. Providing this positive communication should be done often, but a simple "good job" is not enough. Like any other important, one-to-one interaction, positive feedback should be meaningful. To provide the most substantial feedback, consider the following model to gain a deeper level of performance impact.

The Positive Reinforcement Model

Positive reinforcement for high performance has three steps:

- State the exact action or behavior that you want to reinforce. Be specific.

- State the impact that behavior has on you and others.

- State how this action or behavior reflects the person's strengths and character.

A short, effective statement of positive reinforcement might look like this: "Annie, the marketing materials you developed for our new product launch are beautiful and compelling. I believe that anyone who sees them will immediately want to know more about what we do. Your passion and belief in our work, combined with your personal creativity and unfailing pursuit of excellence, are a major factor in our continued growth."

There it is. *Behavior—Impact—Character*. It's not complicated, and it doesn't take a lot of time (perhaps twenty seconds?). But the resulting motivation and behavior can be remarkable. And don't wait until someone has achieved total perfection to offer positive reinforcement (mostly because total perfection generally doesn't happen). Positive reinforcement is paying attention to progress, then rewarding and encouraging it, so that the person is even more highly motivated to continue that action or behavior. And it not only affects and encourages the noted action or behavior but also raises the individual's confidence, inciting people to achieve higher performance in other areas.

Take a minute right now to think of someone who has worked hard to progress in his or her career or at home. Make a few notes using the model and provide positive reinforcement directly and sincerely to that person. It will make him or her feel valued and motivated, even if the person you reinforce doesn't outwardly show it. And it will make you feel even better.

Constructive Feedback

Most high performers (ninety-five-percenters) would agree with this: *good people want to get better.*

That's where constructive feedback comes in. It's feedback that is, well, constructive (construct means to build, right?). It's used when a high performer (a ninety-five-percenter) can make a change that would make him or her *even better*. People frequently say they are uncomfortable providing constructive feedback—to anyone. And it can feel particularly difficult if the communication is directed at your manager or a peer. But in a high-performance environment, it's a responsibility that leaders must embrace, and it's a responsibility for team members who are also part of a high-performing team. If you were teaching a close friend how to play a new sport (golf, tennis, crossbow) at which you were proficient, wouldn't you tell your friend about the little changes and adjustments that would help improve proficiency at, and subsequently his or her enjoyment of, the sport? If good people want to get better, and constructive feedback leads to improved performance, why don't leaders engage in it more often? (Many, in fact, actively avoid it.)

> Most high performers (ninety-five-percenters) would agree with this: *good people want to get better.*

The biggest reason leaders avoid constructive feedback is that they are uncomfortable giving it. The receiver of the feedback could get upset or defensive or have his or her feelings hurt. It could create conflict.

Following are steps that will guide you through the constructive feedback process until you get comfortable with it.

The Constructive Feedback Model

- **Be specific about improvements that can be made.** Generalities aren't helpful. They're the opposite of "good job." It's hard to take specific action on a generality.

- **Be two-sided.** Constructive feedback usually doesn't address major performance issues (those require more consequential, adult-to-adult conversations). Start with identifying what is positive about the person's performance. Don't make this long or flowery or embellished—just acknowledge that many aspects of the person's performance are very good. Remember, constructive feedback is a tip for even better results.

- **When you transition from the positive points to the issue you want to address, don't use the word "but."** People quit listening, and the positive things that you've previously said are negated as soon as they hear the word "but." (*"However," "although," "on the other hand"* are just fancy ways to say *"but"*—so don't use them either.) You can simply replace "but" with "and," or just pause and start a new sentence.

- **Always address the issue, not the person.** Avoid words or sentences that reflect on people's possible weaknesses or their character or their personality.

- **After you have named the specific behavior you wanted to address, ask for the person's thoughts**. You can simply say, "What do you think?"

- **And finally, offer your suggestions, but only if needed.** Usually, the person can figure out how to address the issue or decide if it's worth addressing. Just bringing it to a high performer's attention is appreciated and has the intended impact: trying to make a good person even better.

Other Guidelines for Maximum Impact

- The constructive feedback model is helpful and becomes more streamlined as trust increases between the two people. Sometimes it can be a simple word or a gesture. When cofacilitating our workshops, our team members are continuously giving each other positive and constructive feedback. Because trust and familiarity come from working together for years, they are much briefer in the process. After Bob has presented a segment in the workshop, Mike, the cofacilitator, could tell him, "Bob, you hit every learning point in that section, *and* I think your presentation could have been even stronger if you had delivered it at a faster pace. What do you think?." Instead, during the presentation, Mike simply moves his hand in a circular gesture from the back of the room. (Bob has been known to respond with a gesture of his own.)

- Constructive feedback is easier to give when you have the mindset that *good people want to get better.* Wouldn't you want feedback that could help you be even better at most anything you do? So do your team members.

- Don't talk too much. Make your observation brief and ask what the person thinks. That's it.

- Ken has often pointed out that people don't have to agree with you to have heard you. Some people striving for perfection may initially view constructive feedback as criticism. That's OK. It is not important that you be right or argue until your point is accepted. Give the person a chance to think about it. And as trust grows, the perception of criticism transitions to the belief that you are trying to help him or her get better.

- If you think the person may be hurt or upset (even given the mindset that good people want to get better), it can be helpful to ask first if somebody would like feedback. Usually, the answer is, "yes."

The integration of the elements in the previous chapters is the foundation for creating a high-performance organization. Implementing these seven elements will create a great place to work, a great reputation for the company in the community, and a committed and loyal workforce. Setting high expectations is the final element that is the catalyst for accelerating organizations to new levels of high performance.

Remember: "Do the best you can" limits achievement. People are capable of more. Much more.

The Letter of the Law versus the Spirit of the Law, Part Two

Sam was on fire. He'd had dinner last night with Gloria, a longtime friend who also worked in Human Resources at another company. Gloria was currently engaged in working with the executive team at her company, facilitating the company's transition to a High-Performance Work Place. Some of the biggest changes that would be required affected the HR function and Gloria was excited—as well as a little concerned—about some of these changes. Sam and Gloria had discussed these issues at length. Near the end of dinner, Sam shared his frustration with Rhoda. Gloria emphasized that one of the changes she was responsible for was rewriting all the traditional job descriptions into high-performance job profiles. Being familiar with HR jobs, Gloria helped Sam rewrite Rhoda's job description with an emphasis on responsibility and outcomes instead of tasks and activities.

Sam met with Rhoda the next day and started the conversation by saying that he wanted to consider a different kind of description for her job. He gave her a copy of what he and Gloria had developed. The new job profile was only one page. Rhoda read the first line, which stated the purpose of the job: To assure employees receive the maximum value from company programs and benefits in a safe and welcoming environment.

Three major responsibilities followed below that:

- Ensure every employee feels highly valued through the prompt and accurate resolution of all questions and concerns through open, two-way, adult-to-adult communication.
- Create an environment in which management seeks and trusts advice that is provided to enhance and inspire both employee and leadership performance.
- Uphold and support company and departmental policies while continuously being a champion for ideas and actions that creatively challenge and enhance those policies.

Sam told Rhoda that he believed she could meet these high expectations. While highlighting the functions she was good at, Sam also provided constructive feedback on her role in supporting management and employees in a more positive way. While the job, as now described, seemed somewhat intimidating, Rhoda realized it was much more valuable than she had previously understood. It would take some time and coaching for her to reach Sam's, and her own, expectations, but she now had the confidence, motivation, and belief in herself that would allow those expectations to come to fruition.

MAKING IT
HAPPEN

Creating and sustaining a High-Performance Work Place doesn't have to be a wish or an aspiration. Implementing and living the eight elements is an attainable goal for leaders who want to make change happen and maximize their organization's performance. And it can't be pursued as a *program*, as are many other culture and leadership change initiatives. Programs have a beginning and an end. This is a change in *mindset*—changing the way leaders view the people who make up their companies, and how those people view each other.

It's Not That Complicated

Early in the book, it was stated that creating a high-performance workplace is just not that complicated. We presented eight chapters—one on each of the elements—in which the application of those elements explicitly challenged traditional practices. So now you may be thinking that creating this type of work environment sounds great, but is hard to do alone. What if the rest of the company doesn't support it?

This book was written with the clear intention that readers will act in a different way after evaluating their own beliefs and assumptions and behaviors. Take a minute and look at the elements from the perspective of what can be and cannot be controlled. Whether or not you're in a leadership position, to make any changes, you must feel you have the power to make a difference.

Look at the list of the eight elements on the following page and see if you agree with what elements most people say they can personally control—or at least strongly influence.

Element	Can Control or Influence	Can't Control or Influence
Positive Assumptions About People	✔	
Identification and Elimination of Negatives	✔	
Mutual Trust and Respect	✔	
Open, Two-Way, Adult-to-Adult Communication	✔	
Employee Engagement	✔	
Training	✔	
Competitive Wages and Benefits		✔?
High Expectations	✔	

So, what about *positive assumptions about people*? Most would say that they *can* control this. And because assumptions drive behavior, operating from *positive* assumptions is critical for the implementation of the remaining elements.

What about *eliminating negatives*? Remember that a *negative* is anything that makes another person feel less valued (it's not just something someone doesn't like). Think about the policies and practices discussed earlier that exist only to protect a company from the five-percenters, but are equally applied to everyone (facilities, parking spaces, etc.). Do these policies and practices often apply to the workforce, but not to management? And if so, what can you do about it? Some companies have eliminated these negatives. But if you work in an organization that still makes some employees feel like second-class citizens, you must find ways, as a leader or a contributor, to challenge and influence this change.

What did you answer for *mutual trust and respect*? You may have checked that you can't control it because of the word *mutual*, and it sounds rational to say that you can't control someone else's behavior. One of Ken's hallmark tenets is that *you can't let someone else's behavior dictate yours*. You can control how you interact with people, and when you're consistently trusting of others, trustworthy, and respectful, the majority of those with whom you interact will respond in kind. (Again, don't let that five-percenter dictate your behavior or your level of trust and respect.)

Information is sometimes withheld from the work population at large. Whatever your role in the organization, you can be an advocate for thoughtful and trusting transparency. In your interactions with people, *facilitate* instead of telling or directing. Ask questions and listen to ideas and responses. Be respectful—use a tone of voice and body language that demonstrates openness and respect. You can always control your own adult-to-adult communication style.

Most respondents say that they can control *employee engagement,* even if they're not in an official leadership position. Engagement is strengthened with the incorporations of two-way communication, positive assumptions, trust, and high expectations. As stated earlier, this is *not* a program. It's how small startup companies work and interact before growth and expansion propel them to stifling levels of bureaucracy. When it comes to engagement, just do it. Get started. It's a win/win. Team members win because they have ownership and decision-making authority. Leaders win because they are freed from the daily run and can focus on growth and improvement opportunities.

Many organizations feel that they make a solid investment in *training*. That just makes good business sense. But if they don't, what can they do? If you are a leader, you can be a teacher and a mentor. You can personally be aware of every team member's career desires and the level of their job satisfaction, then create continuous opportunities for individual development. If you are a coworker, you can be proactive in teaching and sharing successful work processes with others.

The arena of *competitive wages and benefits* is one area that people frequently say that they can't control, believing that this is the domain of senior management or the Human Resources department. When it comes to pay, you know if you are personally being treated fairly, and you can certainly find that out through minimal investigation. If turnover in a position is high, you can make a business case for change if the cause of the turnover is paying below market value. Remember that competitive pay is a clear demonstration of the company's fairness and trust.

While some of the elements may call for you to exercise influence (versus having total control), setting and communicating *high expectations* is an absolute requirement for leading and working in a high-performance organization. If someone is doing just the minimum, leaders can control how that minimum is defined. They can raise it. They can coach and inspire everyone around them to rise to their potential. Remember that setting, communicating, and following through on high expectations will *guarantee* higher performance.

When you look at these elements, you can see that you *can control or influence* most of them. A little later, you will be presented with easy and uncomplicated ways to positively affect your organization, the people with whom you work, and most of all, you.

I Am Everyone

Think back to your first job and the jobs you've had since. You can easily remember the things that your boss or the organization did that made you feel angry, frustrated, or devalued. You can also remember the pride you felt in yourself, your team, and your company when you had great work experiences—when you were valued.

In all these ways, everyone is *just like you*. Everything you have experienced, or want to experience, in a great work environment—happiness, reward, pride, recognition—are the same experiences everyone wants. Whether it's an administrative assistant, a production worker, a buyer, a customer service representative, a truck driver, a first-line supervisor, or a senior executive, the desire for trust and respect is not any different. In its simplest, most uncomplicated form, working in a high-performance environment is everyone treating others the way they want to be treated. Or, as Ken says, doing the right thing is always the right thing. And being valued and valuing others *is* the right thing.

> . . . everyone is *just like you.*

Personal Accountability

Mark Samuel is a well-respected author who has published several books on the power of personal and organizational accountability.

In his work, he encourages people to forget about old definitions of accountability because these old definitions often cause people to resist accepting accountability. People resist because they are afraid of being blamed, failing, or even of being successful (since this now becomes the new bar from which they could fail). Mark defines accountability simply as this: "Taking action consistent with your desired outcome."[5] Notice that he states it is *your* desired outcome, not the outcome that someone else has requested. He goes on to say that it's doing what you say you are going to do. It's about making choices.

It's empowering and freeing to know that you are the one who can choose to make a difference in your life and the lives of others. If you are dissatisfied with any of your current work situations, first form an intention of what you want to do to make it better. And don't let the circumstances dictate the outcome—you are in charge of your own desired outcome.

Some Simple Things

Whether or not you're in a formal leadership position, you can do your part in creating a high-performance workplace by taking the following actions:

1. Make time to get to know people. Spend just twenty minutes with each of the people you work with. Ask them to share an important moment in their lives and then share one of your own with them.

2. Seek opportunities to give positive reinforcement. Use the model.

---

[5] Samuel, Mark. *Making Yourself Indispensable: The Power of Personal Accountability.* New York: Portfolio/Penguin, 2012.

3. Give constructive feedback. Remember, *good people want to get better.* If giving constructive feedback makes you uncomfortable, use the model.

4. Make your workplace a fun place to be. Ken says that there was never a day in an HPWP company when he didn't laugh.

5. Insist on high levels of trust with everyone. You are working with responsible adults who own homes, raise children, manage bank accounts, coach their kids' sports teams, serve in their churches, and support their communities.

6. Promote respectful and open communication that will foster that trust.

If you're in a formal leadership position, nothing is more important than creating a high-performance environment, and team, within your sphere of influence. You can control, or at least influence, the eight elements within that sphere.

1. Spend most of your time on developing and inspiring the people you lead. The performance results will be significantly higher than if you spend most of your time in the weeds or in the daily run. (Ken reminds us: The coach doesn't play the game.)

2. Look at how high expectations are communicated (for attendance, performance, and behavior) and raise the bar with the positive belief that people will reach it.

3. Inspire commitment through involving people in every decision that involves or affects them.

4. Set a vision that, at the end of the day, every team member feels valued and that they have spent their time at work in a meaningful way and are looking forward to the next day. (It's the same way you want to feel.)

5. For policy changes, maximize transparency and use your influence for applications over which you don't have complete control. That's what a leader does.

Results matter and improved results get attention. Confidently and calmly go about building your team. Be the model. Set the standard.

The level of high performance you and your team achieve is up to you. The road map is there for you to follow. You may experience a bump or bottleneck or unintended detour along the way. But if you are unwavering and committed to your intent—to make your organization the model of high performance—the road is open.

We would love to see you at your destination.

ABOUT THE **AUTHORS**

Sue Bingham is the founder of HPWP Group. She and her team have coached leaders across all industries, providing guidance that maximizes business performance by valuing people. She created and designed HPWP's signature High Performance Leadership Workshop—an experience that has significantly impacted people's business and personal lives. Sue lives with her husband and mentor, Ken, along with their dogs in Rome, GA.

Bob Dusin was raised on a wheat farm in western Kansas and has worked as a construction manager, human resources and training director, and business owner. For the past fifteen years, he has collaborated with a diverse group of organizations to help create the most engaged and committed workforces possible. He is a member of the National Speakers Association and enjoys work as a radio and television voice actor and an improv comedy performer.

ACKNOWLEDGMENTS

So many people have significantly influenced our efforts in writing this book, and we want to especially thank the following:

Henry DeVries and his wonderful team at Indie Books International, for helping new authors put their passion into words.

Michael Hauge, who taught us how to tell a story in a way that makes our thoughts and experiences impactful and memorable.

The hundreds of leaders who, every day, work to create high-performance workplaces where people can thrive. Through your daily demonstrations of the high-performance principles, you are growing your organizations' success and making this world a better place. You continue to inspire us to passionately spread this message.

Our HPWP team: Annie, Bonnie, Gloria, Jenna, Mike, and Zia. Your unwavering loyalty and dedication to our mission and vision move our words and values into action. We wouldn't be here without you.

And finally, Ken, who has shared his experiences and wisdom in a fun and challenging way—for this we are eternally grateful. Not only have you empowered us to bring positive change and high performance to workplaces, but your guidance and leadership have also enriched both our business and personal lives.

WORKS **CITED**

Gallup, Inc. "State of the American Workplace." Gallup.com. February 15, 2017. http://news.gallup.com/reports/178514/state-american-workplace.aspx.

Pfeiffer, J. William and John E. Jones, Editors. *A Handbook of Structured Experiences for Human Relations Training*, Volume I, Revised. San Diego, CA: University Associated, Inc., 1974.

Semler, Ricardo. "Managing Without Managers." *Harvard Business Review*. August 01, 2014. https://hbr.org/1989/09/managing-without-managers.

Semler, Ricardo. *Maverick!: The Success behind the World's Most Unusual Workplace*. London: Arrow, 1994.

Samuel, Mark. *Making Yourself Indispensable: The Power of Personal Accountability*. New York: Portfolio/Penguin, 2012.

33277440R00095

Printed in Great Britain
by Amazon